Back in the Days of Jesus:
Gospel Homilies
for Children

John

©1996 by Living the Good News, Inc.

All rights reserved. No part of this publication may be reproduced or transmitted in any form or by any means, electronic or mechanical, including photocopy, recording or any information storage and retrieval system, without permission in writing from the publisher.

Living the Good News, Inc.
a division of The Morehouse Publishing Group
Editorial Offices
600 Grant Street, Suite 400
Denver, CO 80203

James R. Creasey, Publisher

Homilies by Dina Gluckstern and Dirk deVries

Editorial Staff: Joanne Youngquist, Kathleen Mulhern, Dirk deVries, Liz Riggleman,
   Dina Gluckstern, Kathy Coffey
Prepress/Production Staff: Sue MacStravic, Noel Taylor, Val Price, Meg Sandoval Phillips
Cover Design and Layout: Val Price, Sue MacStravic
Illustrations: Marcy Ramsey, Anne Kosel, Ansgar Holmberg, Betsy Johnson, Victoria Bergesen

Printed in the United States of America.

The scripture quotations used herein are from the Today's English Version, ©1992, American Bible Society. Used by permission.

ISBN 1-889108-01-4 (Volume 4)
ISBN 1-889108-04-9 (4 Volume Set)

Table of Contents

Introduction

You invite them forward with a mixture of both joy and apprehension, these children of assorted sizes and ages. Adults shift to allow the escape from cramped pews and closely packed chairs. Small forms drop out into the aisles, then bob forward toward the front of the church, some holding hands, some looking back questioningly at parents. Many grin; others share your apprehension. They surround you, watching you closely, waiting for your smile, your touch, your greeting. You know you take a risk each time you welcome this unpredictable group forward, but you also know, as you settle together at the front of the church, that the next few minutes will be among the most rewarding of your week.

Each parish calls it something different: a children's message, perhaps, or a children's sermon or children's talk. Here we refer to it as a children's homily, a short presentation, based on the day's gospel reading, that invites the children to enter into and experience the story of our faith. Each homily respects the children's own spiritual vitality, urging them to share their experience of God, themselves and each other in an environment of love and safety.

Why offer children their own homily?

Offering a children's homily says to the children: "This is a special time just for you, because *church is for you, too.* Here, in church, you are welcomed, delighted in, treasured, held in our arms as you are held in God's arms." A children's homily extends in a concrete way the embrace of our loving God to include these, God's most vulnerable children. "You are this important to us," is the message, as the children file forward to gather for their homily.

But a children's homily offers the children more than the important affirmation that church is their place, too. A well-prepared children's homily couches the basics of Christian experience in terms the children understand and own. It invites children to experience the truths of scripture from the inside out: Children don't learn *about* Jesus calming the storm, they imagine themselves, frightened and rain-soaked, clinging to the sides of the rocking boat, yearning for safety, holding their breath for the moment when Jesus says "Peace, be still," feeling the relief that Jesus brings to the storms they experience in day-to-day life.

Children don't learn about the comfort of Jesus' hug, they exchange Jesus' hugs with each other, then take those hugs out into the congregation. You get the idea.

And the benefits of a children's homily go farther than the children themselves. If you regularly present children's homilies, you already know how often adults approach you after the service and say, "That was great. I got more out of your children's homily than the regular homily." A children's homily—perhaps *because* it presents its point so simply and clearly, with the added framework of childlike wonder and innocence—can profoundly impress and move. Never underestimate the power of a child's fresh perspective or sudden and unexpected insight.

Many of the adults watching from the pews don't have children, or have little regular contact with small children. The children's homily helps balance their lives with the wonder and delight the children take in these encounters with God and scripture.

In addition, when you present the children's homilies, you model for families, friends and relatives ways to engage the children they love in the journey of faith. Storytelling, movement, songs, games and the use of props and illustrations—all of these explore faith in simple ways that others can use as well. After a month or two of watching children's homilies, people begin to catch on, even unconsciously adopting the methods demonstrated in your children's homilies.

Who are these homilies for?

Back in the Days of Jesus: Gospel Homilies for Children from the Gospel of John contains thirty-seven homilies, written for children from the age of four or five through eleven or twelve. Admittedly, this is a broad age range, and you may find some homilies seem more appropriate for the younger children than the older. We have attempted to provide something for all ages in each homily, including occasionally offering options within the homilies themselves. Keep in mind that a children's homily is not an instructional activity, and that age matters less when sharing in ritual and worship. In fact, a variety of responses can enrich the experience for all participants. You may want to invite older children to help younger children with certain tasks and responses. The older children will benefit from the sense of awe and wonder—the raw spirituality—of the younger children.

These homilies will work for both small and large groups, from less than half a dozen to as many as thirty or more. When appropriate, we suggest ways to change the homily for very small or very large groups; for example, in a large group, you may not be able to invite every child to offer a response to every question; do your best to let different children answer each question. In a small group, you may be able to reproduce a simple prop for each child to take home. For the most part, the size of the group will not matter, but if it does, you should be able to adapt each homily for the number of children you anticipate coming forward.

If you regularly have a larger group (more than twelve), consider recruiting another adult or teenage helper for each additional six or so children. This is particularly helpful when the homily includes more complex activities, or if another leader can provide a calming influence for restless children.

How do I prepare?

Each homily in this book includes:
- a scripture reference
- a quote from the reading
- a brief summary of both the reading and the homily
- a materials list
- directions for the homily
- a suggestion for closing prayer

We encourage you to begin your preparation by reading the scripture on which the homily is based. You might consider reading the story in two Bible versions, including *Today's English Version,* used in the preparation of these homilies. Think about the passage. You might ask yourself:
- What does this reading say to me?
- What truth about God, about others or about myself do I learn from this reading?

Then extend your question to include the children you anticipate will join you for the homily:
- What would I like the children to hear in this story?
- What does this reading say to them about the love and care of God?

After your own consideration of the reading, read through the summary of the reading and the homily,

check the materials list and read once through the homily itself.

Most homilies in this book offer both an age-appropriate retelling of the gospel story and at least one activity to help the children enter into the meaning of the story (occasionally both story and activity are blended into one overall activity). Time limitations or personal preference may require that you use one or the other rather than both. Feel free to do so. The stories can stand alone; if you wish, a question or two taken from the activity may be enough to help you draw a story-only homily to a conclusion. Likewise, you may not wish to retell the gospel story if it has just been read from the Bible or lectionary; in this case, simply follow the regular reading of scripture with the homily activity.

Once you decide how much of the homily you wish to present, gather your materials and practice telling the story. We encourage you to memorize the story, though you may certainly use your own words if you wish. Tell the story to yourself, a friend or a family member once or twice. Inexperienced at storytelling? Familiarize yourself with the two cardinal rules of storytelling—make eye contact with your listeners and make sure they can hear you!

At the conclusion of each homily we offer a prayer. Again, add to or adapt each prayer as you wish.

Some basic principles to keep in mind:
- *The younger the children, the shorter the homily.* One guide-

line suggests that children will sit still and listen one minute for each year of their age; for example, the average five-year-old will be there, attending to you, for five minutes, an eight-year-old for eight minutes. Keep that in mind at points in the homily when you are doing the talking, for example, during a non-participatory story. That's why these homilies incorporate lots of feedback and interaction.

- *There are more people involved than you and the children.* The parishioners listen and participate along with the children. Face the parishioners as you sit down to present the homily. Speak loudly, slowly and clearly. Repeat answers given by children if the children speak too softly for the parishioners to hear. If you use a poster or another prop, make it big enough —and hold it up high enough— for the parishioners to see, too. If children participate in actions (other than in a circle or semicircle facing inward), face them toward the parishioners. While you and the children are not performing for the parishioners, you do invite them to worship with you. Keep that in mind.

- *Respect what children say.* You don't need to correct the children, you need only allow them to experience the story for themselves, to find their own meaning and, if they wish, to articulate that meaning. God reveals God's self to children, as to adults, in the right ways at the right times. Trust God to do this in your children's homilies.

In the homily, affirm all children for their responses; a simple thank-you accomplishes this beautifully. You can also say, "Jared, you believe..." or "Deanna, you feel like..," reflecting back to children what they have shared. Acknowledge each child's right to believe and feel whatever he or she believes and feels without editorializing. At times you may be hoping the children suggest a specific idea; if they do not, simply suggest the idea yourself. Your ideas matter too, and the children want to hear them.

- *Expect the unexpected.* In these homilies you invite open responses from creative, uninhibited children. You cannot control what they say or do (nor would you want to). If they perceive you as a caring friend, they will want to tell you about their pets, toys, eating habits and other topics that you may prefer not to discuss when you are leading in front of your parishioners. This will happen. Expect it, flow with it and enjoy it. Welcome even off-the-wall comments with grace and good humor, but be cautious not to laugh at the children, even when the parishioners do. A child can easily feel hurt if a serious comment shared in trust is met with laughter. Show your respect for the children by responding appreciatively to whatever they say.

Deal with the unexpected comment by acknowledging the child and redirecting attention back to the story or activity. If a child continues, you can thank him or her for the desire to share and explain that now you would like to focus on the activity or story at hand. Ask the child, "May I listen to your story later, after church?" Be sure to follow through with the child later. You might also put your finger to your lips and say, "This is our quiet time, our time to listen to the story. Can you do that for us?"

It always helps to remember: The clearest message to the children does not come through the content of your homily, but through the loving relationship you offer them when you gather together.

On Sunday morning, make sure to bring your collected materials and this book. Take a few minutes for a final review. Place any needed materials unobtrusively near the area where you will gather the children.

We recommend that you gather at the front of the church. Children can sit in a semicircle around you on the floor. If the floor is not carpeted, consider purchasing a large square carpet remnant to make sitting more comfortable. Many churches have several low steps at the front of the church; you could sit on one of these or on a low stool. You could, of course, also sit with the children on the floor.

Once you and the children settle in, begin the homily. Look with love and respect at each young face before you. You are in for a treat: these children have invited you into a most sacred circle. Consider yourself honored...and see what God will do.

Dirk deVries

One final note: Looking for a reading not covered in this volume? That reading may have a parallel in one or more of the other gospels— Matthew, Mark or Luke. Look in the other volumes in *Back in the Days of Jesus: Gospel Homilies for Children* and you may find the homily you seek.

■ ■ ■ ■ ■

John 1:1-18

**In the beginning the Word already
existed; the Word was with God, and
the Word was God. From the very
beginning the Word was with God.
(John 1:1-2, *Today's English Version*)**

Summary

In this reading from the Gospel of
John, the gospel writer describes
Jesus as the pre-existent Word of
God, source of life, light for human-
ity. In today's homily, children first
talk about the importance of light,
then hear and discuss today's story.

Materials

Bible
several candles secured in candle
  holders
matches
several flashlights
a reading lamp with the necessary
  extension cords

Homily

Invite the children to come forward
for today's homily. Ask them to sit
in a semicircle around you.

With the children, discuss:
■ How do we feel at night, when
  it's dark? when we're alone in
  bed with the lights out? when
  we're outside, with a family
  member? when the lights go
  out suddenly for some reason?
  *(Encourage children to add
  their own stories of darkness.)*

■ What kinds of lights do I have
  here with me this morning?

If possible, dim the lights in the
church. Light the candles. Ask:
■ When do we use these kinds
  of lights?

Blow out the candles and turn on
the reading lamp. Ask:
■ When do we use this kind of
  light?

Turn off the reading lamp and distribute flashlights. Let children
shine them around the darkened
church. Collect the flashlights and
ask:
■ When do we use these kinds of
  lights?
■ How do we feel when we see
  light after it's been dark?
■ What difference does light
  make?
■ In today's story, Jesus is called
  "the light." Let's find out why.

Hold the Bible open to the Gospel
of John as you tell today's story:

**Back before there were moms
and dads, grandmothers and
grandfathers, aunts and uncles,
boys and girls...**

Back before there were dogs and cats, horses and cows, snakes and bugs, bees and birds...

Back before there were flowers and weeds, trees and bushes, oaks and pines, thorns and vines...

Back before there were rain and wind, snow and clouds, sunshine and fog, dew and dust...

Back before there were rocks and rivers, stars and planets, cities and oceans, ponds and houses...

Back before there was anything, there was God.

And there was Jesus.

Jesus was with God.

Jesus and God together made all the wonderful things of creation.

Jesus gave life to us.

And Jesus brought light to us.

Jesus' light shines all around us. Jesus' light helps us to do what is right. Jesus' light helps us to follow him. Jesus' light helps us to feel safe and loved.

Jesus' light shines in the darkness. The darkness can not put it out. Jesus' light shines forever...in me *(point to self)*...and in you *(point to each child)*... and in everyone in this church *(point to the parishioners)*.

If you wish, discuss with the children:
- What hard times do we have, when we might feel the way darkness sometimes makes us feel? When do we feel afraid? lonely? sad?
- Today's story told us that Jesus is like a bright light in deep darkness.
- How could having Jesus with us during hard times make a difference to us?
- When are we aware of hard times that others have?
- How can we, like Jesus, make a difference for others during these hard times?

Prayer

- Jesus, thank for shining in our lives like light in the darkness. Thank you for making hard times easier. *Amen.*

Thank the children for joining you and invite them to return to their seats.

John 1:6-8, 19-28

John answered by quoting the prophet Isaiah: "I am 'the voice of someone shouting in the desert: Make a straight path for the Lord to travel!'" (John 1:23, *Today's English Version*)

Summary

In this reading from the Gospel of John, John the Baptist announces the coming of the Messiah. In today's homily, children play a game of Who Am I?, then hear today's story and talk about ways to welcome Jesus.

Materials

Bible

Homily

Invite the children to come forward for today's homily. Ask them to sit in a semicircle around you.

Play Who Am I? with the children. Begin by silently choosing an identity for the children to guess, perhaps a popular cartoon, children's book or TV character. Explain:

- Let's play a game of Who Am I?
- I'm thinking of a character from a cartoon (or a book or TV program) whom I think you know.
- You can ask me as many questions as you like to try to figure out who I am, but only questions that I can answer with yes, no or maybe.
- Who am I?

Let children ask questions. Give hints, if necessary, to move the game along. When children have guessed your identity, say:

- The people of Jesus' time were very puzzled when a man came out of the desert preaching.
- They kept asking the man, "Who are you?"
- That's the story I want to tell you today.

Hold the Bible open to the Gospel of John as you tell today's story:

God sent a messenger to the people. The messenger was a man. The man's name was John.

John came to the people and started preaching. "Turn from your sin," he said. "Follow God!" John baptized people in the river. "Get ready for God. God is coming!"

People scratched their heads. What is he talking about, they

13

wondered. Several people approached John. "Who *are* you?" they asked him. "Are you the light of God?"

"No, I'm not the light of God," said John.

"Then who *are* you?" they asked again. "Are you the prophet Elijah, from long, long ago?"

"No, I'm not the prophet Elijah, from long, long ago," said John.

"Then who *are* you?" they asked again. "Are you the Messiah, promised by God?"

"No, I'm not the Messiah promised by God," said John.

"Well, then, *who are you?*"

John answered: "I am a voice.

"I am a voice shouting in the desert.

"I am a voice telling you about the light of God.

"I am a voice telling you to prepare the way for Jesus, the Messiah.

"I am a voice saying, 'Get ready! He is coming!'

"I am the one who baptizes you, getting you ready for the coming of Jesus."

The people looked at one another. They started to smile. They felt excited. "The Messiah is coming," they said to each other. "The light is coming! Jesus is coming!"

"How shall we prepare?

"How do we get ready for the coming of Jesus?

"How shall we get ready for Jesus?"

Ask the children:
■ How can we get ready for Jesus?

Invite many responses from children before concluding with today's prayer.

Prayer

■ Jesus, come to us and be with us. As John welcomed we welcome you. *Amen.*

Thank the children for joining you and invite them to return to their seats.

■ ■ ■ ■ ■

John 1:29-41

"There is the Lamb of God!" he said.
(John 1:36b, *Today's English Version*)

Summary

In this reading from the Gospel of John, John the Baptist identifies Jesus as the "Lamb of God," and Jesus is joined by his first disciples. In today's homily, children hear today's story, explore what it means that Jesus is the Lamb of God, and symbolically give their "troubles" to Jesus.

Materials

Bible
modeling clay
toothpicks
large paper sack

Before the homily create several "pricklies" for each child. To create a prickly, roll a lump of modeling clay into a ball about 1/2" in diameter. Break four or five toothpicks in half and stick the broken ends of the toothpick into the clay.

Homily

Invite the children to come forward for today's homily. Ask them to sit in a semicircle around you.

Hold the Bible open to the Gospel of John as you tell today's story:

John the Baptist sees Jesus coming. He says to his friends, "Jesus is the Lamb of God."

The Lamb of God? his friends wonder. What does John mean?

Then they remember:

They remember a story about another lamb, the story of Abraham and Sarah, who never had a child until they were old. How they loved little Isaac, the child of their old age. With joy they watched him grow.

Then one day, Abraham heard God tell him, "Take your son Isaac whom you love to a mountain. Then give him to me."

Abraham was afraid and sad. But he took Isaac to the mountain.

"Where is the lamb we will give to God?" Isaac asked.

"God will give us that lamb," Abraham said.

And on the mountain, God did. God blessed Abraham and promised long life to Isaac. God showed Abraham a sheep, caught in the bushes, that Abraham could give to God. Abraham and Isaac went home together.

"Jesus is the Lamb of God," the people hear John say.

The people remember another story, a story of another lamb, the story of the first Passover. God's people were slaves in Egypt. God sent Moses to take the people away from Egypt, so they could be free.

God told the people to eat a special meal: roasted lamb and quickly-made bread. "Eat it standing up," God said, "with your shoes on your feet, ready to walk away from Egypt forever."

Every year God's people ate this special meal, and remembered how God had made them free.

"Jesus is the Lamb of God," the people hear John say.

Two of John's followers hear John call Jesus the Lamb of God. From then on they follow Jesus.

Explain to the children:
- John said that Jesus was the Lamb of God, who takes away the sin of the world.
- That means that Jesus takes away the hurts of the world, too, like our loneliness, sadness, anger and fear.

- What are some times when we feel lonely, sad, angry or frightened?

Give each child several of the "pricklies" prepared before the homily. Hold up one prickly and explain:
- This is a prickly.
- I like to pretend each prickly is one of the things I feel sad, angry or frightened about.
- This prickly, for example, is my fear of... (name something you fear.)
- I'm going to give my prickly— my fear of (name fear)—to Jesus by dropping it into this paper bag. I'll let Jesus have it; he'll help me take care of it.

Offer two more examples of personal pricklies before dropping them into the paper sack. Then invite children to do the same, identifying areas of life that are scary, upsetting, lonely, sad or angry, until all the pricklies have been thrown away. Say:
- I'm going to throw our pricklies away.
- That's my way of remembering that Jesus cares about all our pricklies, and wants to help us with all of them.

Prayer
- Jesus, you are the Lamb of God, who takes away life's pricklies. Thank you. *Amen.*

Thank the children for joining you and invite them to return to their seats.

■ ■ ■ ■ ■

John 1:43-51

Philip found Nathanael and told him, "We have found the one whom Moses wrote about in the book of the Law and whom the prophets also write about. He is Jesus son of Joseph, from Nazareth." (John 1:45, *Today's English Version***)**

Summary

In this reading from the Gospel of John, Jesus calls Philip and Nathanael to be his disciples. In today's homily, children first hear this story, then listen as each of them in turn is called to come and follow Jesus, too.

Materials

Bible
optional:
paper
pen or pencils

Homily

Invite the children to come forward for today's homily. Ask them to sit in a semicircle around you.

Before beginning the story, be certain that you know the names of all the children who have come forward. If you don't, take a moment to write down their names. You will be calling each child by name at the conclusion of the homily.

Hold the Bible open to the Gospel of John as you tell today's story:

Jesus knew: It was time to start teaching and healing. I will walk a lot, he said to himself. And I will be in strange towns meeting new people all the time. It will be lonely, all by myself.

Then Jesus had an idea: I will ask people to join me. They can walk with me. They can learn from me, and I will have friends to help me.

Jesus talked to two brothers, Simon Peter and Andrew. Jesus invited them to join him; "Come with me," he said. So Simon Peter and Andrew followed Jesus.

Jesus saw a man named Philip, visiting at the synagogue. "Come with me," Jesus said to Philip, and Philip followed Jesus, too.

Philip found his friend Nathanael as Nathanael rested under a fig tree. Philip said to Nathanael, "I've met the Messiah. His name is Jesus. He comes from the town of Nazareth."

Nathanael laughed. "Nazareth? Nothing good comes from Nazareth!"

"Come and see," answered Philip.

When Jesus saw Nathanael, he said. "Here's the one who says just what he thinks...even about Nazareth!"

Nathanael's mouth dropped open. "How did you know about that?" he asked.

Jesus answered, "Nathanael, I saw you sitting beneath the fig tree when Philip invited you to meet me."

"You are the Son of God!" Nathanael said to Jesus. "You are the Messiah!"

Invite a child to play the part of Jesus for the remainder of the homily. Ask that child to stand at the front of the church, perhaps on a step or low stool.

Ask the other children to scatter around the church, up the aisles and across the front and back. Have Jesus call each child by name, using this invitation:
■ (Name), come follow me!

As each child is called, he or she comes forward to stand by Jesus.

When all the children have been called forward, consider continuing with the names of several adults or older children seated in the church.

Conclude by inviting the entire group, including all parishioners, to say in unison:
■ We are all called to follow Jesus!

Prayer

■ Jesus, thank you for calling each of us to follow you, just like you called Simon Peter, Andrew, Philip and Nathanael. *Amen*.

Thank the children for joining you and invite them to return to their seats.

■ ■ ■ ■ ■

John 2:1-11

Two days later there was a wedding in the town of Cana in Galilee. Jesus' mother was there, and Jesus and his disciples had also been invited to the wedding. (John 2:1-2, *Today's English Version***)**

Summary

In this reading from the Gospel of John, Jesus performs his first miracle, turning water into wine at a wedding. In today's homily, children first discuss pictures of parties, then participate in the telling of the gospel story.

Materials

Bible
photographs of parties and celebrations, for example, weddings, birthdays, holiday dinners, etc.
6 small clay or pottery jars (see *note* below)

Note: If you can't find six small clay jars or containers, you can quickly make simple jars from modeling clay. Either pinch balls of clay or coil thin ropes of clay into jar shapes:

Homily

Invite the children to come forward for today's homily. Ask them to sit in a semicircle around you.

Use the party pictures as a focal point for a discussion about celebrations. Hold up the pictures, one at a time, and ask:
■ What's happening in this picture?

Encourage the children to talk about what they see in the pictures and what they remember from such celebrations they have attended. You can extend the discussion by asking:
■ What do people eat at these kinds of parties?
■ What do people drink at these kinds of parties?
■ What do people wear to these kinds of parties?
■ What makes these kinds of parties fun?

Explain:
■ Parties are special times of happiness and celebration.
■ Jesus liked parties, too! He helped make a party extra

special, and that's the story I want to tell you today.

Hold the Bible open to the Gospel of John as you tell today's story. Invite the children to join you in making the accompanying motions and "hums":

One day, Mary, Jesus and Jesus' friends all went to a wedding.

At the wedding, there was a bride and groom. At the wedding, there was music to hear. *(Hum a few happy notes.)*

At the wedding, there was good food to eat. *(Rub your stomach.)* **At the wedding, there was good wine to drink.** *(Pretend to taste wine from a jar.)*

And at the wedding, there were clay jars—clay jars to hold water—clay jars waiting. *(Line up the jars in front of you.)*

Everyone danced to the music. *(Hum.)* **Everyone ate the good food.** *(Rub your stomach.)* **But before everyone could drink the wine...the wine was gone! There was no more wine to drink.**

"Help them, Jesus," said Mary. "They need more wine."

Jesus saw the clay jars—clay jars to hold water—clay jars waiting. *(Touch each jar.)*

"Fill these jars," said Jesus. People filled the jars with water. *(Pretend to fill each jar.)*

"Now drink," said Jesus. People drank. *(Pretend to drink.)* **But they didn't drink water. They drank wine. Jesus had changed the water to wine!**

"Delicious!" said the people. "Jesus, this is the best wine of all."

If you wish, discuss with the children:
- Jesus went to a special party and had fun. How did Jesus make this party extra fun?
- What parties do you like?
- What do you like to do at parties?

Prayer

Invite the children to thank God for parties and things they like to do. Close by praying:
- God, thank you for parties—and for Jesus, too. Thank you for miracles and all your signs of love to us. *Amen*.

Thank the children for joining you and invite them to return to their seats.

John 2:13-22

He made a whip from cords and drove all the animals out of the Temple, both the sheep and the cattle; he overturned the tables of the moneychangers and scattered their coins... (John 2:15, *Today's English Version*)

Summary

In this reading from the Gospel of John, Jesus drives the merchants from the Temple and predicts his death and resurrection. In today's homily, children first hear the story, then dramatize and discuss Jesus' actions in the temple.

Materials

Bible

Homily

Invite the children to come forward for today's homily. Ask them to sit in a semicircle around you.

Hold the Bible open to the Gospel of John as you tell today's story:

Jesus went with his friends to the temple. He wanted to worship God. He knew in the temple, people prayed to God. In the temple, people sang to God. In the temple, people learned about God. In the temple, people offered to help each other in the name of God.

But when Jesus arrived at the temple, guess what he found? Jesus saw people selling cattle. He saw people selling sheep. He saw people selling doves. People were buying and selling and making change. They had turned God's temple into a big supermarket!

"This is not what the temple is for!" Jesus said to his friends.

Jesus felt angry. He took some rope and made a whip. Then he chased everyone out of the temple, along with their cattle and sheep and doves. He turned over the tables, and money scattered everywhere.

Jesus said to the people who were buying and selling, "Don't make God's house a marketplace! This is the place to worship God!"

The disciples saw Jesus' anger. They remembered something Jesus had said before: "My love for God's house burns in me like a fire!" Now they understood. **Jesus loved God's temple. Jesus loved to worship God. Jesus wanted everyone to be able to worship God, whether in the temple, a synagogue or a church.**

Invite children to act out today's story.

Recruit a single volunteer to play the part of Jesus. Then recruit groups of volunteers to play the parts of the animal sellers, the money changers and the bystanders. Let children enact the cleansing of the temple.

After several minutes of noisy role-playing, ask the children to be seated. Discuss:
■ Imagine that you really were one of the animal sellers, the money changers or the bystanders.

Now it's evening and you've gone home to eat dinner with your family. Someone asks you, "What happened at the temple today?" How do you answer?
■ What was Jesus saying to us? How did we answer?
■ These days we come to church to worship God. What parts of our time together at church do you like best?

Prayer
■ Jesus, thanks for letting us know how important it is to come together to worship God. Help us to worship God together this morning. *Amen.*

Thank the children for joining you and invite them to return to their seats.

22

■ ■ ■ ■ ■

John 3:1-17

"How can a grown man be born again?" Nicodemus asked. "He certainly cannot enter his mother's womb and be born a second time!"
(John 3:4, *Today's English Version*)

Summary

In this reading from the Gospel of John, Jesus meets secretly with Nicodemus, answering the Pharisee's questions about his ministry. In today's homily, children hear this story and talk about the questions they would like to ask Jesus.

Note: If you are looking for a homily specifically based on John 3:16, see the homily for John 3:14-17, on page 25.

Materials

Bible
newsprint or poster board
felt marker

Homily

Invite the children to come forward for today's homily. Ask them to sit in a semicircle around you.

Invite the children to share questions they would like to ask Jesus:
- Imagine that Jesus was here with us this morning.
- What questions would you want to ask Jesus?

Record the children's ideas on newsprint or poster board. Encour-

age an atmosphere of acceptance, emphasizing that all of the children's questions are worthy of attention and respect.

Hold the Bible open to the Gospel of John as you tell today's story:

Once there was an important man named Nicodemus. He was a leader of God's people. He taught others in the temple. Many people came to Nicodemus to ask him questions, and learn from his wisdom.

But one day Nicodemus learned of a teacher named Jesus. Jesus was different from all the other teachers to whom Nicodemus listened. Nicodemus wondered, "Who is this Jesus? What special message does he have from God?"

Nicodemus was afraid to see Jesus during the day. Many teachers were angry at Jesus, and Nicodemus did not want these teachers to be angry at *him*, too.

But he wondered more and more about Jesus. So one night, when it was dark and no one

could see him, he went to Jesus. He had so many questions to ask.

"Are you really from God?" he asked. "Do you really do God's work?"

Jesus listened to Nicodemus' questions, and answered them. He told Nicodemus, "No one can go into God's kingdom unless they are born again."

"Born again?" asked Nicodemus. "What does that mean? Grownups can't become little babies again."

"That's not what I mean," Jesus answered. "I mean people must start a brand-new life, with God's power. People must learn to love the way God loves."

"But how can this happen?" Nicodemus asked. Jesus was teaching him brand-new things, and this made Nicodemus ask even *more* questions.

"God makes this happen," Jesus said. "God helps people start a brand-new life through the power of God's own Spirit."

Nicodemus wanted to know still more. "Why have you come to us from God?" he asked.

Jesus knew this was a very important question, and he gave a very important answer: "God has given me to you, so that everyone who believes in me may have eternal life. That's how much God loves you!"

Invite children to recall the questions they would like to ask Jesus. Discuss:
■ What questions did Nicodemus have for Jesus?
■ What answers did Jesus have for Nicodemus?

Explain:
■ The most important answer that Jesus gave Nicodemus is this: God loved the world so much that God gave Jesus to us, so that we all might live with God forever.
■ God loves each one of you so much, that God would have sent Jesus to you if you were the only person in the whole world.

Prayer
■ Thank you Jesus, for answering Nicodemus's questions. Please answer our questions, too. *Amen*.

Thank the children for joining you and invite them to return to their seats.

■ ■ ■ ■ ■

John 3:14-17

"For God loved the world so much that he gave his only Son..." (John 3:16a, *Today's English Version*)

Summary

In this reading from the Gospel of John, Jesus summarizes the heart of the good news, that God loved the world and sent Jesus to save it. In today's homily, children discuss the meaning of Jesus' death.

Materials

Bible
crucifix or artwork depicting Jesus on the cross
large cross created of cardboard (Cut apart cardboard boxes and tape the pieces together to form a cross; make the cross at least 4'-5' high; reinforce the cross with duct tape, wooden dowels or thin strips of wooden lath.)
crayons and colored felt markers

Homily

Invite the children to come forward for today's homily. Ask them to sit in a semicircle around you.

Hold the Bible open to the Gospel of John as you tell today's story:

It was dark, late at night. Jesus was still awake, sitting outside so he could enjoy the cool evening air, the stars and the gentle breeze.

A man suddenly appeared out of the darkness. "Psst," he said. "Jesus?"

"Yes?" said Jesus.

"May I talk with you?" asked the man.

"Certainly," said Jesus. "But why are you being quiet?"

"Because some of my friends don't want me talking with you."

"Oh," said Jesus. He waited for the man to continue.

"Jesus, you speak of the Kingdom of God. You talk about eternal life. How can I find God's Kingdom? How can I get eternal life?"

Jesus rested his hand on the man's shoulder. "To find God's Kingdom," he said, "you must believe in me. To get eternal life, you must follow me."

And then Jesus said, "God has given me to you, so that everyone who believes in me may have eternal life. That's how much God loves you!"

Later, the man watched Jesus die on a cross. He remembered

what Jesus said...that God had given Jesus so that everyone who believes in Jesus would have eternal life.

Show the crucifix or other artwork to the children and discuss:
- Who is this pictured on the cross? Who can tell us why Jesus is pictured on the cross?
- Crucifixion—hanging on a cross—was one way in which criminals were killed in Jesus' time.
- Jesus was considered a criminal because he stood up for what he believed in.

Display the cardboard cut in the shape of a cross. Ask:
- What is this I have made?
- That's right, a cross. What is our cross made of? What do you think Jesus' cross was made of? *(wood)*
- Because Jesus loves each of us so much, he gave his life for us, dying on a hard wooden cross. That was a very scary thing for Jesus to do. That was a very sad time for Jesus' friends. What do you imagine that was like for Jesus and his friends?
- Let's say a quiet thank-you to Jesus for loving us enough to die. *(Reverently say, "Thank you, Jesus," together with the children.)*
- We may never give our lives for someone else, but everyday, we can give to others. Can you think of times when people have given up things to help other people?

If children need help thinking of examples of sacrifice, remind them of those who give food to the hungry, clothes to the homeless and time to the needy. Older children may also understand those who donate organs or blood, missionaries who give up comfortable lives to help the poor in other countries, people who open their homes to those suffering with AIDS, and people who risk their reputations (or even lives) to support unpopular causes.

After a number of examples have been shared, lay the cardboard cross flat on the floor, make available crayons and colored markers, and invite children to gather around the cross, each child writing or drawing on the cross one way in which people sacrifice for others and for God.

Read aloud or describe the children's additions to the cross as they work for the benefit of the parishioners. When children have finished, lift the cross for all to see. Say:
- The story of Jesus and the cross doesn't end with Jesus' death.
- What happened just a few days after Jesus' died?
- That's right, God raised Jesus to new life. Jesus is alive today! What do you think about that?

Prayer

- Jesus, thank you for dying for us on the cross. Thank you for living with us today. *Amen.*

Thank the children for joining you and invite them to return to their seats.

■ ■ ■ ■ ■

John 3:23-30

"This is how my own happiness is made complete. He must become more important while I become less important." (John 3:29b-30, _Today's English Version_)

Summary

In this reading from the Gospel of John, John the Baptist acknowledges that his ministry must now give way to that of Jesus. In today's homily, children hear today's story and discuss how they feel when other people get special treatment.

Materials

Bible
snack to share with children

Homily

Invite the children to come forward for today's homily. Ask them to sit in a semicircle around you.

When the children have settled down, ask two children to come and with you, one on each side. Give these children a snack and invite them to eat it. Observe the other children and discuss:
■ How do you feel when someone gets a snack, and you do not?
■ How do you feel when someone gets invited to sit beside the teacher, and you do not?
■ The friends of John the Baptist once asked him questions just

like these, and that's the story I want to tell you today.

Give each child a snack before continuing. Hold the Bible open to the Gospel of John as you tell today's story:

John the Baptist spent the whole day preaching and baptizing. "Repent!" he told the people. "Turn from your sin. Follow God."

John led people into the shallow water of the river and poured water over them. "The Messiah is coming. Follow him," he told them.

John felt tired. His voice was hoarse from talking, talking, talking. The sun was setting and the sky was a rosy red, streaked with clouds. John sighed in relief. "Time to stop for today," he said to his followers.

A few minutes later they relaxed together on the bank of the river, sharing bread. Some of John's followers came up and dropped beside him. "Teacher," they said, "We have

something important to tell you. Remember that man Jesus, the one whom you baptized in the Jordan River?"

"Yes," said John, for he remembered Jesus very well. He knew Jesus was God's Messiah, God's chosen one.

"Well," continued John's friends, "he's baptizing now, too! People are going to see him instead of you! What shall we do about it?"

John sighed again. He felt even more tired. "If people are going to see Jesus, then God is with Jesus. Jesus' words come from God. Jesus' touch comes from God. Jesus is baptizing for God."

"But what will happen to you?" asked John's followers.

"I came to point the way to Jesus," John answered. "He must become more important while I become less important. This is what God wants. I am glad for Jesus. Be glad for Jesus, too."

With the children, discuss:
- Why were John's friends worried?

- How do you think John's friends felt about Jesus?
- How did John feel about Jesus?
- Sometimes it is hard to be happy for other people when good things happen to them. We want good things to happen to us, too.
- Do you remember how you felt when I asked these two children to sit with me? when I gave them each a treat?
- John was glad when he heard that people wanted to see Jesus. Why do you think John felt that way?
- I wonder if we can be happy when good things happen to our friends, even if those good things don't happen to us.

Let children respond to this final "I wonder..." if they wish. Be realistic about their responses. A healthy amount of self-focus is appropriate for young children. Don't expect them to give this up because of today's homily, but do expect them to consider the possibility of rejoicing in the blessings of others, even if they don't share those blessings themselves.

Prayer

- Jesus, help us to be glad, as John was glad, to know that good things happen to others, too. *Amen*.

Thank the children for joining you and invite them to return to their seats.

John 4:5-42

Jesus answered, "If you only knew what God gives and who it is that is asking you for a drink, you would ask him, and he would give you life-giving water." (John 4:10, *Today's English Version***)**

Summary

In this reading from the Gospel of John, Jesus' request for water from a Samaritan woman results in many new believers in the woman's town. In today's homily, children first share cold water, then hear today's story.

Materials

Bible
large pitcher of cold water
small paper cups

Homily

Invite the children to come forward for today's homily. Ask them to sit in a semicircle around you.

Pour cups of water for those who want them. Ask:
- When do we especially want a cup of cold water to drink?
- When do we like to splash or play in water?
- On what kinds of days do we like to watch water coming down like rain?
- When we see others thirsty, what do we want to do for them?

Explain:
- Jesus once longed for a cold cup of water himself.
- That's the story I want to tell you today.

Hold the Bible open to the Gospel of John as you tell today's story:

Once Jesus and his friends were walking to the land of Galilee. They came to a town called Sychar in the land of Samaria. Jesus' friends went into the town to buy food, but Jesus was hot and tired. He sat down next to a well to rest.

He saw a woman come near. She was a Samaritan woman. Now Jesus was a Jewish man. Jews did not speak to Samaritans at all. They wouldn't even use the same cups or bowls that Samaritans used.

But Jesus paid no attention to these rules.

When the woman got to the well, Jesus said to her, "I'd like a drink of water."

The woman looked up in surprise. "But you are a Jew," she said, "and I am a Samaritan. You shouldn't even be talking to me! And you're asking me for a drink?"

Jesus answered, "If you only knew what God could give you, right now, you'd forget about the drink of water and ask *me* for a drink of *life-giving* water."

"Life-giving water?" the woman asked. "That sounds like something the Messiah would give."

Jesus answered, "I am he, I who am talking with you."

The woman left her big water jar there by the well and ran back into town. To everyone she met she said, "There's someone special at the well. Come and see him. I think he might be the Messiah, God's special messenger!"

Many people left the town and went back to the well with her to see Jesus.

The people of the town begged Jesus to stay with them, so he stayed there two more days, talking with them.

Explain:
- Hearing good news about Jesus can feel as good as drinking a cool glass of water when you are very, very thirsty.
- The Samaritan people were very glad when the woman told them the good news that Jesus was the one God had sent to them.
- What good news about Jesus do we know?
- What good news about Jesus can we share?
- How can we share good news about Jesus with others?

Prayer

- Jesus, your good news felt like cool, clear water to the Samaritan woman and her friends. Help us to know and share the good news, too. *Amen.*

Thank the children for joining you and invite them to return to their seats.

John 6:4-15

Jesus took the bread, gave thanks to God, and distributed it to the people who were sitting there. (John 6:11a, *Today's English Version*)

Summary

In this reading from the Gospel of John, Jesus feeds more than five thousand people with just five loaves of bread and two fish. In today's homily, children first sample good food that God gives us, then hear today's story.

Materials

Bible
basket
5-6 food items (see **note** below)
knife
paper plates
napkins

Note: **Before the homily** gather five or six food items in a basket. Chose items that will appeal to a variety of the children's senses.
Examples:
■ sense of sight: shiny red apple or deep brown nuts
■ sense of smell: onion, garlic or roasted peanuts
■ sense of touch: rough coconut, prickly pineapple
■ sense of taste: any fresh or dried fruit

Homily

Invite the children to come forward for today's homily. Ask them to sit in a semicircle around you.

Begin the homily by showing children the food items, one by one. Invite children to look at, touch and smell each one. Encourage children to share stories about their favorite foods. Let children have sample bites of one or more items. Say:
■ Today's story is about food, too.

Hold the Bible open to the Gospel of John as you tell today's story:

The boy sat on a grassy hillside and looked around him. Thousands of people sat nearby. He had never seen so many people in one place in his whole life. And they were all there to listen to a new teacher named Jesus.

"God loves you," Jesus said. "So love one another, too."

Silence hung over the crowd. Two women hugged one another. A man sitting next to the boy sat with his eyes closed, not sleeping, but thinking.

Then a few people got up to stretch. "Look how late it's

grown," one man said. "We really need to feed the children."

"And us!" said his wife. The boy suddenly realized how hungry he was. He was glad his mother had wrapped up five loaves of barley bread and two fish for him to eat.

But when he looked around him, he couldn't see any other baskets like his. What would everyone eat?

He heard one of Jesus' friends say, "Jesus, to feed this many people, we would need more than two hundred silver coins to buy enough bread."

The boy got up and ran to Jesus' friends. He tugged at the robe of the man called Andrew. "Sir, I have some bread—and some fish, too. Jesus can have that to feed these people."

Andrew smiled as he looked into the basket. "Two fish and five loaves of bread? That won't feed five thousand people, but you are good to give it. Thank you."

Andrew took the basket to Jesus. Jesus looked up and smiled, right at the boy. Then he said to Andrew, "Have the people sit down."

As the people sat, Jesus took the bread into his hands. "Blessed are you, O Lord our God, King of the Universe, for you have brought forth bread from the earth," he prayed.

He broke the bread and gave it to his friends to pass among the people. Then he blessed the fish and shared that food, too. All the people—every single child, woman and man—took bread and fish and ate until they could eat no more. There was more than enough!

"Gather up what's left," said Jesus to his friends. The friends walked through the crowds with baskets. They filled twelve baskets with the food that was left.

"How can this be?" the people asked one another.

The boy looked at his small empty basket and at the twelve baskets filled to overflowing. Then he looked at Jesus. What had Jesus said? "God loves you, so love one another, too," the boy whispered.

He picked up his basket and slowly walked down the hill toward home.

If you wish, discuss with the children:
- What good food did Jesus give the people in today's story?
- What good food does God give us, every day?

Prayer

- Thank you, Jesus, for feeding the hungry people. Thank you, God, for feeding us every day. *Amen*.

Thank the children for joining you and invite them to return to their seats.

John 6:24-35

"Do not work for food that spoils; instead, work for the food that lasts for eternal life." (John 6:27a, *Today's English Version*)

Summary

In this reading from the Gospel of John, Jesus tells those seeking to be fed by another miracle (such as the feeding of the five thousand or the giving of manna from heaven) to come and "feed on" him and his teaching. In today's homily, children hear today's story, then brainstorm all the different ways they can think of to learn about and from Jesus.

Note: If you're looking for a children's homily that explores Jesus' role as the "bread of life," see the homily for John 6:37-51, on pages 35-36. If you're looking for a homily with a eucharistic emphasis, see the homily for John 6:53-59, on pages 37-39.

Materials

Bible
large sheet of poster board
felt marker

Before the homily title the poster board *Learning about Jesus.*

Homily

Invite the children to come forward for today's homily. Ask them to sit in a semicircle around you.

Hold the Bible open to the Gospel of John as you tell today's story:

The people crowded around Jesus. He had done an amazing thing. Jesus had taken just five little loaves of bread and two fish, and with them fed more than five thousand people! That's more people than we have in church this morning... *with only five loaves of bread and two fish!* **No wonder the people felt excited. No wonder they crowded around Jesus.**

The people wanted to see another miracle. "Do it again, Jesus!" they cried. "Feed us some more! Here's a bunch of grapes; can you make twelve baskets full? Here's a roasted leg of lamb; can you make a whole lamb out of it?"

Jesus shook his head. "I'm glad you had enough to eat, but now you follow me only to see another miracle. But I'm not here

to work miracles and give you food.

"I bring something even better than miracles and food. I bring eternal life."

Eternal life? The people looked at each other. That sounded even better than miracles. That sounded better than lots of food. "Tell us, Jesus," they asked, "how do we get this life."

"Believe in me," Jesus said. "Listen to me. Follow me. Learn from me. Then you will have food far better than the bread and fish you ate a little while ago. You'll have something to last throughout this life...and beyond."

Show children the poster prepared **before the homily**. Discuss:
- Who would like to read what our poster says?
- That's right, it says, *Learning from Jesus.*
- Jesus said that learning from him is very important, more important than his miracles.
- Let's try to think off all the different ways we can learn about Jesus.

Invite children to suggest ideas. As each idea is suggested, write—or, if possible, draw—that idea on the poster. Keep in mind that many of the children are not yet readers; drawing a picture of a Bible, repre-

senting Bible stories, will make more sense for these children than writing the word *Bible.* If you consider yourself a non-drawing homilist, you may be able to recruit a drawing partner **before the homily**.

Remember to repeat suggestions for the benefit of the parishioners if children speak softly.

If children need help getting started, share one or more of these suggestions:
- We learn about Jesus from hearing the Bible read in church.
- We learn about Jesus from Bible stories read to us at home.
- We learn about Jesus from the songs we sing about Jesus.
- We learn about Jesus from what our parents and friends tell us about Jesus.
- We learn about Jesus' love from the care we receive from people who love us.
- We learn about Jesus by helping others.

Prayer
- Jesus, help us always to keep learning about you and knowing you better and better. *Amen.*

Thank the children for joining you and invite them to return to their seats.

John 6:37-51

"I am the bread of life. Your ancestors ate manna in the desert, but they died. But the bread that comes down from heaven is of such a kind that whoever eats it will not die." (John 6:48-49, *Today's English Version***)**

Summary

In this reading from the Gospel of John, Jesus describes himself as "the bread of life," bread that brings eternal life. In today's homily, children first share and discuss bread, then draw a parallel between their daily need for food and their daily need for Jesus.

Note: If you're looking for a children's homily with a Eucharistic emphasis, see the homily for John 6:53-59, on pages 37-39.

Materials

Bible
pita or other flat bread

Homily

Invite the children to come forward for today's homily. Ask them to sit in a semicircle around you.

Begin the homily by tearing the bread into bite-sized pieces and giving one piece to each child. As the children eat the bread, discuss:
■ What are we eating?

■ What does this bread taste like?
■ What other kinds of bread do we like?
■ When do we eat bread?
■ How often do we eat bread?
■ What would we miss most if we never again had bread to eat? Would we miss sandwiches? toast with butter and jelly? crackers with cheese?
■ In some parts of the world, people eat even more bread than we eat. If they didn't have bread, they would go hungry.
■ Back in the days of Jesus, bread was very important too. When Jesus and his friends didn't have bread, they went hungry too.
■ Maybe that's why Jesus said what he said about bread in today's story. Let's listen.

Hold the Bible open to the Gospel of John as you tell today's story:

The people crowded around Jesus. They felt excited. He had done an amazing thing. Jesus had taken just five little loaves of bread...like the one we just shared...and two fish, and with them fed more than five thou-

sand people! That's more people than we have in church this morning...with only five loaves of bread and two fish! No wonder the people felt excited. No wonder they crowded around Jesus.

The people wanted to see another miracle, but Jesus wanted to give them something better than bread and fish...he wanted to give them himself.

So Jesus said to the people, "I am the bread of life."

"What?" asked the people. "You are bread? But Jesus, you don't *look* like a loaf of bread!"

Jesus answered, "I am the bread of life. I don't mean that I'm made of bread, I mean I am like bread for you.

"Do you need bread everyday?" Jesus asked.

"Yes," said the people.

"Then you need *me* everyday, too. And does eating bread help you do you work, play together and stay strong and healthy?"

"Yes," said the people.

"I help you do your work, play together and stay strong and healthy, too. And do you enjoy eating your bread every day?"

"Yes," said the people.

"Then enjoy spending time with me every day, too. I am the bread of life. I am as important to you, everyday, as the bread you eat. Feed on me. Listen to me. Follow me. Live close to me.

"I am the bread of life," said Jesus.

Prayer

■ Jesus, bread of life. Be with us every day. Feed us. Love us. *Amen*.

Thank the children for joining you and invite them to return to their seats.

John 6:53-59

"This, then, is the bread that came down from heaven; it is not like the bread that your ancestors ate, but then later died. Those who eat this bread will live forever."
(John 6:58, *Today's English Version*)

Summary

In this reading from the Gospel of John, Jesus explains that he is food and drink for eternal life. In some parishes, children partake of the Eucharist; in other parishes this is not the case. Today's homily, therefore, encourages children to view all of their time in church as an opportunity to be "fed by Jesus." Children first discuss the use of vestments, vessels and wafers in church, then hear today's story and learn a simple song about attending church.

Note: If you're looking for a children's homily that explores Jesus' role as the "bread of life," see the homily for John 6:37-51, on pages 35-36.

Materials

Bible
optional:
Eucharistic vestments
chalice and paten
unconsecrated wafers

Homily

Invite the children to come forward for today's homily. Ask them to sit in a semicircle around you.

If you have brought vestments and vessels, let the children examine and touch these. Let the children taste the unconsecrated wafers. Discuss:
■ What are these?
■ When do we see these used in church?

If vestments, vessels and wafers are not available, invite the children to discuss:
■ What special clothes does the priest wear at the Eucharist?
■ What special dishes do we see during the Eucharist?
■ What do people eat at the Eucharist?

Introduce today's story by saying:
■ Jesus feeds us in many ways, not just at the Eucharist, and that's the story I want to tell you today.

Hold the Bible open to the Gospel of John as you tell today's story:

Jesus brings us together in church. Jesus feeds us at church to show us that he loves us.

We put on special clothes to go to church. The priest puts on special clothes, too. Are you wearing special clothes this morning? *(Pause for children's responses.)*

We come into church. We greet God with a song. Let's greet

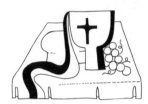

God together now. *(Sing with the children:)*

> Good morning to you,
> Good morning to you,
> Good morning, dear Father,
> Good morning to you.
>
> Good morning to you,
> Good morning to you,
> Good morning, dear Jesus,
> Good morning to you.
>
> Good morning to you,
> Good morning to you,
> Good morning, dear Spirit,
> Good morning to you.

It feels good to greet God.

We hear God's word in church, too. We hear stories about Jesus, like this one. What stories do you know about Jesus? *(Pause for children's responses.)* It feels good to hear stories about Jesus.

We give our gifts of money in church, too. We give our gifts of bread and wine. It feels good to give to God.

We give God thanks. What would we like to thank God for this morning? *(Pause for children's responses.)* It feels good to give thanks to God.

(Modify this paragraph to fit the practice of your parish:) We eat God's bread. What do you think about as you eat God's bread? *(Pause for children's responses.)* It feels good to eat God's bread.

We go home knowing that Jesus has fed us. We go home knowing that Jesus loves us. *(Say this slowly, looking directly into the eyes of each of the children.)* It feels good to be loved by Jesus.

With the children, sing these words to the tune of "Here We Go 'Round the Mulberry Bush." Make the suggested motions to accompany the song, and encourage the children to make the motions with you. You might invite the parishioners to join you, as well:

This is the way we go to church,
   go to church,
   go to church.
This is the way we go to church,
   so early in the morning.
(Walk the fingers of one hand in the palm of the other hand.)

This is the way we greet the Lord,
   greet the Lord,
   greet the Lord.
This is the way we greet the Lord,
   so early in the morning.
(Cup hands around mouth as you sing.)

This is the way we hear God's
    word,
    hear God's word,
    hear God's word.
This is the way we hear God's
    word,
    so early in the morning.
(Cup a hand behind one ear.)

This is the way we eat our bread,
    eat our bread,
    eat our bread.
This is the way we eat our bread,
    so early in the morning.
*(Hold our your hands as if you
are receiving the Eucharistic
bread.)*

This is the way we go from church,
    go from church,
    go from church.
This is the way we go from church,
    so early in the morning.
*(Run and skip the fingers of one
hand in the palm of the other.)*

Prayer

■ Thank you, Jesus, for feeding us
each week at church. *Amen.*

Thank the children for joining you
and invite them to return to their
seats.

39

John 6:60-69

Simon Peter answered him, "Lord, to whom would we go? You have the words that give eternal life. And now we believe and know that you are the Holy One who has come from God." (John 6:68-69, *Today's English Version*)

Summary

In this reading from the Gospel of John, Jesus struggles with the faithlessness of some of his followers while affirming the life-giving quality of his words. In today's homily, children first hear today's story, then share some of Jesus' "words of life."

Materials

Bible

copies of the Words of Life sheet, 1 per child (see **before the homily** note below)

Words of Life poster (see **before the homily** note below)

Before the homily make photocopies of the Words of Life sheet printed at the end of the homily to distribute at the conclusion of today's homily. You will need one copy per child.

Also **before the homily** prepare a Word of Life poster to use during the homily. Select two or three of the "word of life" statements found on the Word of Life sheet found at the conclusion of today's homily. Copy these statements in large letters on a large sheet of poster board.

Homily

Invite the children to come forward for today's homily. Ask them to sit in a semicircle around you.

Hold the Bible open to the Gospel of John as you tell today's story:

"Jesus! The things you teach are just too hard! We don't understand! We give up!" The followers of Jesus were angry.

Jesus looked at his followers with sad eyes. "You want to give up?" he said. "My words might

be hard, but they are the truth. My words are God's words. My words give life."

But Jesus' followers would not listen.

"I just want to hear good things. I don't want to have to make hard choices." One man went home.

"I don't believe what you tell us. You don't know what you are talking about." A woman went home.

Many people left, but Jesus' disciples, his closest friends, stayed. Jesus looked at them and wondered.

"Do you, my disciples, want to leave, too? Are my words too hard for you, too?"

The disciples looked at each other. Finally Peter said, "Where else would we go? Jesus, you are the only one who can teach us about life. Your words give life to us." The other disciples agreed.

Jesus felt glad his disciples were so ready to listen and to learn. Truly, they were his best friends.

Show children the poster you prepared **before the homily**. Ask:
■ Jesus said that his words bring life. What do you think Jesus meant?
■ Sometimes, Jesus words bring me comfort when I feel frightened or sad or alone. That is one way Jesus' words bring life.
■ I've written two (or three) of Jesus' life-giving words on this poster. Can someone read one of them for me?

After the statement is read, discuss:
■ How do you feel when you hear these words of Jesus?
■ How do these words give life?

Repeat for the other one or two statements written on your poster. Continue:
■ Here is a sheet of paper on which you will find several of Jesus' life-giving words. You can take these home with you. If you can't read yet, that's okay; ask a friend or family member who can read to read these words with you, especially when you feel lonely, sad or afraid.

Distribute one Words of Life sheet to each child.

Prayer
■ Thank you, Jesus, for your wonderful words of life. *Amen*.

Thank the children for joining you and invite them to return to their seats.

■ ■ ■ ■ ■

Words of Life
(from the *Today's English Version*)

Jesus said: "Happy are those who mourn; God will comfort them!" (Matthew 5:4)

Jesus said: "You are like light for the whole world." (Matthew 5:14a)

Jesus said: "Ask, and you will receive; seek, and you will find; knock, and the door will be opened to you." (Matthew 7:7)

Jesus said: "Come to me, all of you who are tired.., and I will give you rest." (Matthew 11:28)

Jesus said: "I will be with you always, to the end of the age." (Matthew 28:20b)

Jesus said: "Let the children come to me, and do not stop them, because the Kingdom of God belongs to such as these." (Mark 10:14)

Jesus said: "Everything is possible for God." (Mark 10:27b)

Jesus said: "My words will never pass away." (Mark 13:31b)

Jesus said: "I am the good shepherd. I know my sheep and they know me." (John 10:14-15)

Jesus said: "I will ask the Father, and he will give you another Helper, who will stay with you forever." (John 14:16)

Jesus said: "I love you just as the Father loves me..." (John 15:9)

Jesus said: "I do not call you servants any longer... I call you friends..." (John 15:15)

John 9:1-38

"One thing I know: I was blind, and now I see." (John 9:25b, *Today's English Version***)**

Summary

In this reading from the Gospel of John, Jesus heals a man born blind, then defends his actions against the attack of the Pharisees. In today's homily, children first discuss changes they would like God to help them make in their lives, then hear today's story.

Materials

Bible

Homily

Invite the children to come forward for today's homily. Ask them to sit in a semicircle around you.

Discuss with the children:
- If we could ask Jesus to change just one thing in our lives, what would we ask?

Encourage many different answers to this question.

Be careful to create an accepting atmosphere as children talk. For example, children may well wish that their baby brothers or sisters would not live with them anymore. We can accept the children's remarks as accurate statements of their feelings, without expressing either approval or disapproval.

Example:
- You wish that you didn't have a baby brother in your family.

Say:
- Jesus once made a big change in the life of a man who could not see, and that's the story I want to tell you today.

Hold the Bible open to the Gospel of John as you tell today's story:

Jesus and his friends were walking near the temple, when they saw a blind man. This man had been blind ever since he was born. He had never seen anything at all.

Many teachers in Jesus' day taught that this was because the man or his parents were sinners. These teachers said, "God punished this man or his parents by making him blind."

Jesus' friends asked Jesus, "Is this true?"

Jesus said, "No. God did not make him blind because he was a sinner. God did not make him blind because his parents were sinners. And today God will make him see again."

"Today?" asked his friends. "But today is the Sabbath and no one is supposed to work on the Sabbath."

"Today," said Jesus. "I will do God's work."

Jesus spat on some dirt. He made the dirt and spit into mud. He rubbed the mud on the man's eyes, and told him to go wash his face.

The man did what Jesus said, and an amazing thing happened—he could now see. He wasn't blind anymore.

People were amazed at what Jesus had done, but the teachers were angry. They questioned the man again and again. They told him that Jesus must be a sinner, too, for working on the Sabbath.

The man said, "No. He comes from God. He made me see."

But the teachers sent the man away from the synagogue. He could see now, but he could never worship with his friends and neighbors again.

When Jesus heard what had happened, he found the man. Jesus asked him, "Do you believe in the Son of Man?"

"Who *is* the Son of Man?" the man answered.

Jesus said to him, "You are looking at him now. I am the Son of Man."

"I believe, Lord!" the man said, and knelt down before Jesus.

Ask children to recall the changes they brainstormed earlier in the homily. Discuss:
- What did Jesus change for the man in today's story?
- What problems did the man still have? *(Teachers still believed he was a sinner and sent him away from the synagogue.)*
- Imagine Jesus made the changes in our life that we wanted. What problems would we still have in our lives?

Explain:
- God's power can change our lives and change the world we live in.
- One way God's power can change lives is when we make changes in our lives.
- What are some ways we can work on some of the problems in our lives? *(Encourage children to brainstorm practical problem-solving behaviors, for example, in handling family conflicts.)*

Prayer

- Jesus, thank you for healing the man who could not see. Thank you for helping us make good changes in our lives, too. *Amen.*

Thank the children for joining you and invite them to return to their seats.

■ ■ ■ ■ ■

John 10:1-10

Jesus said, "I am telling you the truth: the man who does not enter the sheep pen by the gate, but climbs in some other way, is a thief and a robber. The man who goes in through the gate is the shepherd of the sheep." (John 10:1-2, *Today's English Version***)**

Summary

In this reading from the Gospel of John, Jesus likens himself to the gate for a sheep pen, as well as the shepherd whose voice the sheep listen for and follow. In today's homily, children first learn a chant to use in the telling of today's story, participate in the story and then practice "listening for the voice of the shepherd."

Materials

Bible

Homily

Invite the children to come forward for today's homily. Ask them to sit in a semicircle around you.

Teach the children this chant, emphasizing the syllables printed in boldface:

I **am** the Good **Shep**herd;
my **sheep** follow **me**.

It may help the children to learn this chant if they clap in rhythm—clapping on the boldfaced syllables—as they chant.

Explain to children that you will add lines from today's Bible story between each chant. Hold the Bible open to the Gospel of John as you tell today's story:

I am Jesus, the Good Shepherd; I care for my sheep.

I am the Good Shepherd; my sheep follow me.

The sheep hear my voice; I call my own by name.

I am the Good Shepherd; my sheep follow me.

I bring them out of their pen and go ahead of them.

I am the Good Shepherd; my sheep follow me.

They will not follow someone else; they do not know his voice.

I am the Good Shepherd; my sheep follow me.

Others come to destroy, but I will bring you life.

I am the Good Shepherd; my sheep follow me.

Ask the children to stand together in a circle. Choose one child to be the first shepherd and two other children to be the first two thieves. Ask the shepherd and thieves to stand in the center of the circle. Make certain that the children in the outer circle understand which child is the shepherd and which two children are the thieves, then ask the circle of children to turn and face outward. Explain:
- Let's pretend that the inside of our circle is a sheep pen, and that the rest of us are sheep.
- In a moment, the shepherd and both of our thieves will invite you to turn and enter the sheep

pen. Can you recognize the voice of the shepherd? If you think the shepherd invited you in, turn around and step forward. If you think one of our two thieves invited you in, stay right where you are.

First let the two thieves invite the sheep into the sheep pen, then the shepherd. If children are mistaken and turn on either of the first two invitations, simply ask them to turn back and wait for the shepherd's voice.

Repeat a time or two with other children playing the shepherd and thieves; vary the order in which the shepherd and thieves make their invitations to the sheep.

Stand together in a circle and, if you wish, ask:
- How do you think we hear the voice of our Good Shepherd, Jesus?

Prayer
- Jesus, help us to listen for your voice. *Amen.*

Thank the children for joining you and invite them to return to their seats.

■ ■ ■ ■ ■

John 10:11-16

"I am the good shepherd." (John
10:14a, *Today's English Version*)

Summary

In this reading from the Gospel of
John, Jesus describes himself as the
good shepherd, who knows his
sheep and is willing to die for
them. In today's homily, children
search for missing sheep, then hear
today's story.

Materials

Bible
6 cotton balls or 6 sheep figures
    from a creche set or play farm
sheep pen *(see directions below)*

Directions for sheep pen:
■ Make a stack of six frozen treat
   sticks.
■ Pull out every other stick 1/2".
   You should have a stack of sticks
   in which three sticks extend to
   the left and three sticks extend
   to the right.
■ Use two rubber bands to secure
   the stack.

■ Make at least five stacks.
■ You can join the fences together
   into a sheep pen by interlacing
   fences at the ends.
■ Form the joined fences into a
   sheep pen or other shape.

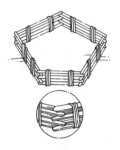

Before the homily hide five of
the six cotton balls or sheep figures in the area at the front of the
church where you will be gather-
ing with the children. Place them
so they can be easily found by the
children.

Homily

Invite the children to come forward for today's homily. Ask them
to sit in a semicircle around you.

Begin today's homily by talking
briefly about sheep. Ask:
■ What sounds does a sheep
   make?
■ What do you call a baby sheep?
■ What colors are sheep? *(Sheep
   come in many shades of gray,
   tan, brown and black, in addition to white.)*

Set up the sheep pen. Place the
remaining (sixth) cotton ball or
sheep figure just outside of the
sheep pen and say:
■ Here's a pen for sheep, but only
   one of the sheep is here. There
   are five other sheep, and they
   are lost.

■ Can you help me find the five other sheep? They're hiding around us here at the front of the church.

Invite children to find the missing sheep. When all five have been retrieved, ask children to place them around the outside of the sheep pen. Say:

■ Jesus once talked about sheep and shepherds, and that's the story I want to tell you today.

Hold the Bible open to the Gospel of John as you tell today's story:

The sheep are in the field. There is good grass for them to eat and clean water for them to drink. The sun shines on their wool, and they feel happy when the breeze cools their muzzles.

Their helper brings them fresh hay to eat.

One sheep leaps up in fear and begins to bleat. "Baaa! Baaa!" The other sheep stumble to their feet and look.

A wolf! The sheep turn to run, but their turning takes them in every direction. They trip and bump, not knowing where to go. The hungry wolf draws closer.

Some sheep run to the helper. He can save them! But the helper sees the sharp teeth of the wolf. He turns and runs, far, far away. "Baaa! Baaa!" The bleating grows loud; the wolf crouches to spring.

"Get away!" yells a voice. A wooden crook smashes the ground, and the wolf leaps away. The sheep's bleating grows joyful. The shepherd has come! He knows how to save his sheep. The wolf slinks away from the strong voice and heavy crook. The sheep tumble around the legs of their beloved shepherd.**

"It's all right, Curly Horn," he calls out. *(Move one sheep into the sheep pen.)* "Here, Black Ear, come to me." *(Move a second sheep into the sheep pen.)* He knows his sheep by name. "Don't be afraid, Molly." *(Move another sheep into the pen.)* And his sheep know him. "You are safe, now, Spot and Nanny." *(Move two more sheep into the pen.)* "There you go, Fluff." *(Move the last sheep into the pen.)* The sheep draw close and the shepherd comforts them.

***(Pause and look at the children as you say:)* Jesus says to us, "I am your Good Shepherd. You are my sheep. I call each of you by name. I know you and you know me."**

I wonder how Jesus knows us. I wonder how we can know him.

If children wish, allow them to respond to your final "I wonders..."

Prayer

■ Jesus, thank you for being our Good Shepherd. Thank you for caring for us like a shepherd cares for sheep. *Amen.*

Thank the children for joining you and invite them to return to their seats.

■ ■ ■ ■ ■

John 10:27-30

"My sheep listen to my voice; I know them, and they follow me. I give them eternal life, and they shall never die. No one can snatch them away from me." (John 10:27-28, *Today's English Version***)**

Summary

In this reading from the Gospel of John, Jesus, the Good Shepherd, describes his relationship to us, his sheep. In today's homily, children first take turns being shepherds and sheep, then hear today's gospel story.

Materials

Bible
masking tape, a chair or two, large boxes, rope and/or other items with which to create a simple obstacle course
blindfolds (bandannas, scarves, etc.)

Before the homily set up a simple obstacle course at the front of the sanctuary using a chair or two, several boxes, rope, etc. Use masking tape to mark the start and finish lines.

Homily

Invite the children to come forward for today's homily. Ask several older children to play shepherds and several other children to play sheep. Blindfold the sheep and ask the shepherds to lead the sheep through the obstacle course. Shepherds use their voices only, unless they think a sheep may trip or fall, in which case they may also use touch to guide the sheep.

Repeat with other sheep and shepherds if time allows.

Ask the children to be seated in a semicircle around you. Hold the Bible open to the Gospel of John as you tell today's story:

What do shepherds do?

Shepherds take good care of their sheep.

Shepherds know each one of their sheep by name. "Here, Lambkin! Come and eat, Greyling!"

Shepherds take good care of their sheep.

Shepherds take their sheep to green pastures, where the sheep can graze on fresh, green grass. Shepherds take their sheep to clear, blue pools, where the sheep can lap up clean, fresh water.

49

Shepherds take good care of their sheep.

Shepherds know when even the smallest, youngest sheep gets lost. "Where is Lambkin? I'll go find her!"

The shepherd looks over the hills and across the water and behind the bushes. "Here you are, Lambkin. I found you. Now I'll carry you home."

Shepherds take good care of their sheep.

Jesus is our Good Shepherd.

"I love you, my friends," says Jesus. "I want to take good care of you, just like good shepherds take care of their sheep."

Jesus takes good care of us. Jesus knows each one of us by our names. *(Pause to name each child—and yourself, too.)*

Jesus says, "No matter what you do or where you go, I will always love you. I will always look for you and find you."

Jesus takes good care of us.

Jesus is our Good Shepherd.

Prayer

■ Thank you, Jesus, for being our Good Shepherd. Thank you for taking good care of us. *Amen.*

Thank the children for joining you and invite them to return to their seats.

John 11:1-44

"Jesus said to her, "I am the resurrection and the life." (John 11:25a, *Today's English Version*)

Summary

In this reading from the Gospel of John, Jesus brings his friend Lazarus back to life. In today's homily, children discuss their understanding of death, then hear today's story.

Materials

Bible
newspaper
flowerpot
seeds
potting soil
gravel or pebbles
water
large spoon

Homily

Invite the children to come forward for today's homily. Ask them to sit in a semicircle around you.

As you do the following, invite the children to discuss what you are doing:
- Spread the newspaper.
- Arrange gravel or pebbles in the bottom of the flowerpot.
- Fill the pot three-quarters full of soil, then carefully lay the seeds on the soil.
- Cover the seeds with a layer of soil. Water the soil.

Explain that there are many difficult questions that neither scientists nor other grown-ups understand very well; for example:
- Are the seeds we just planted alive or dead?
- If we never planted or watered them, would they be alive or dead?
- How does life get into a dead-looking seed?

Entertain as many answers as the children are willing to volunteer. Mention that in God's plan, we see both life and death over and over again. Point out examples in nature. If the discussion is going well, continue with the following questions:
- Have any of us ever had a pet or a plant die? Have any of us ever known a person who died? What happened? How did we feel?
- How is life different than death?

Keep in mind that these questions are aimed at provoking thought rather than eliciting "right" answers. To lead into the story, affirm that the line between life and death has always been mysterious.

Hold the Bible open to the Gospel of John as you tell today's story:

Jesus was a man with many friends. He loved them all very, very much.

Three of Jesus' best friends were a man named Lazarus and his sisters, Mary and Martha.

Lazarus, Mary and Martha all lived together in a town called Bethany. Jesus liked to visit his friends at their home in Bethany. Together they would talk about God and pray.

One day a messenger ran to Jesus, where he was staying with his disciples. "Jesus," the messenger cried out. "Your friend Lazarus is very sick. Mary and Martha want you to come right away."

But Jesus did not rush to where Lazarus lay sick. Jesus waited for two days before he made the trip.

When he finally arrived near Bethany, he was met by Martha. She was angry and crying as she said, "You are too late. Lazarus died four days ago. We have already buried him in a tomb."

"Do not be afraid," said Jesus. "Remember how we have talked together about God's power? You will see God's power this very day."

When Mary heard that Jesus had come, she ran to meet him. She was so sad she could not say a word to Jesus, but fell at his feet and cried aloud.

Jesus was heartbroken to see Martha and Mary so sad. He cried with them. He asked them to show him where Lazarus was buried. Mary and Martha took Jesus to Lazarus's tomb, a cave with a stone in front of the opening.

"Take the stone away!" Jesus ordered.

They rolled the stone away and Jesus spoke again. "Lazarus—come out!"

Martha and Mary did not know where to look. At Jesus? at the tomb? What could they possibly see?

But then Martha whispered, "Look! Oh, Mary, look!" She pointed to the door of the tomb. There was Lazarus, still wrapped in his burial cloths, but walking out of the tomb—alive!

Mary and Martha were so amazed they couldn't even move until Jesus said gently, "Take away his burial cloths. Let him walk freely now that he is alive."

And that is all the Bible tells us. We do not know what happened next. Did they sit to eat together? Did Lazarus want to tell Mary and Martha what it had been like to be dead? Did Mary and Martha want to tell Lazarus how much they had missed him?

We do not know. I wonder what you think happened next.

Let children respond before continuing with today's prayer.

Prayer

■ Thank you, God, for Jesus and his friends Mary, Martha and Lazarus. Thank you for your gift of life. *Amen.*

Thank the children for joining you and invite them to return to their seats.

John 12:20-33

"Now my heart is troubled—and what shall I say? Shall I say, 'Father, do not let this hour come upon me'? But that is why I came—so that I might go through this hour of suffering." (John 12:27, *Today's English Version*)

Summary

In this reading from the Gospel of John, Jesus speaks about his approaching death. In today's homily, children hear today's story, then learn and repeat a simple action rhyme about Jesus' death and resurrection.

Materials

Bible
poster board
felt marker

Homily

Invite the children to come forward for today's homily. Ask them to sit in a semicircle around you.

Begin the homily by drawing a large cross on the sheet of poster board. Ask:
■ What is this?
■ Let's look around us. Can we see other crosses in the church? Are any of us wearing crosses, as on a necklace, pin or ring?
■ Why do we have crosses around the church? Why do we wear crosses as necklaces or pins?
■ Today's story tells us something about crosses.

Hold the Bible open to the Gospel of John as you tell today's story:

I see a cross *(trace the arms of the cross on the poster)* and I think of what Jesus once said: "The hour is coming when I will die on the cross."

Jesus cried.

Jesus prayed.

"I am so troubled, God," said Jesus. "What shall I say? Shall I say, 'Don't let this happen, God?' But if I die on the cross, your promise will come true. All people will be God's people.

"All of them, from the oldest to the youngest, the richest to the poorest, the smartest to the simplest will know God and love God. And they will know that God loves them."

Jesus cried.

Jesus prayed.

"God, save me, even if I die," said Jesus.

And God answered Jesus and said, "I will."

I see a cross *(again trace the arms of the cross on the poster)* and I think of love.

Jesus died on the cross, but God loved Jesus. God did not leave Jesus to death. God gave Jesus new life, life that will never end.

And then God gave us new hearts *(lay your hand over your heart)*, full of love. Now all of us are God's people. Now each of us, whether old or young, rich or poor, smart or simple can know God and love God.

And now we can know—God loves us.

Ask children to stand together in a circle. Teach them the words and movements to this rhymed version of today's story:

Jesus bowed
His head and cried,
(Kneel. Put hands on face, as if crying.)

"I'm scared because
I'm going to die.
(Stretch out arms in cross shape.)

But God will give
New life to me,
(Raise arms.)

And all God's people
Will be free."
(Stand. Join hands with neighbors.)

Now Jesus lives,
So happy be!
(Drop hands, hug self and spin in place.)

Because he loves
Both you and me.
(Point to self, then neighbor.)

Prayer

■ Jesus, we are sad that you suffered and died. We are happy that you came back to life. Thank you for loving us so much. *Amen.*

Thank the children for joining you and invite them to return to their seats.

■ ■ ■ ■ ■

John 13:1-20

Then he poured some water into a washbasin and began to wash the disciples' feet and dry them with the towel around his waist. (John 13:5, *Today's English Version***)**

Summary

In this reading from the Gospel of John, Jesus washes the disciples' feet, offering an example of humility and service. In today's homily, children experience foot-washing and participate in a rhymed telling of the story.

Materials
Bible
tubs, dish pans or basins filled with warm water
towels

Homily

Invite the children to come forward for today's homily. Ask them to sit in a semicircle around you.

Say:
■ In today's story Jesus and his friends went to eat a special meal together.
■ Jesus' friends were hot and dusty. They wanted to have their feet washed!
■ Jesus wanted his friends to know how much he loved them. So Jesus washed the feet of each one of his friends.

Invite children to remove their shoes and socks, then to take turns washing and drying each other's feet. Let children wash your feet, too!

Hold the Bible open to the Gospel of John as you tell today's story. Use simple actions to tell today's story with the children:

Jesus and his friends sit down to eat.
(Sit in a circle with the children.)

"First," says Jesus, "I'll wash your feet."
(Each person pretends to wash the feet of the person on his or her left.)

"If I can wash your feet for you, then you can wash each other's feet, too."
(Each person pretends to wash the feet of the person on his or her right.)

Jesus takes wine,
Jesus takes bread.
"Eat these with me,"
Jesus said.
*(Each person lifts right hand,
then left, then pretends to sip
and eat.)*

"Here's a new rule:
Love one another.
I love you,
my sisters and brothers.
*(Each child hugs child on left,
then child on right.)*

"People will know
we are sisters and brothers,
when we do just this:

Love one another."
*(Join in a circle by putting arms
on each other's shoulders.)*

If it feels appropriate, help children shout together the last line of the story.

Prayer

■ Jesus, thanks for washing the feet of your disciples. Help us to show our love for others by doing kind things for them, too. *Amen.*

Thank the children for joining you and invite them to return to their seats.

John 13:31-35

"And now I give you a new commandment: love one another. As I have loved you, so you must love one another." (John 13:34, *Today's English Version*)

Summary

In this reading from the Gospel of John, Jesus issues a "new commandment": love one another. In today's homily, children hear this story, then share examples of ways in which to love others, responding to these examples with a "love" chant based on the story.

Materials

Bible

Homily

Invite the children to come forward for today's homily. Ask them to sit in a semicircle around you.

Hold the Bible open to the Gospel of John as you tell today's story:

Jesus looked around the table. How he loved these good friends who broke bread with him: noisy John and James, brave Thomas, Peter, who always said just what he thought, and so many others.

But all his friends looked puzzled and worried right now. They were thinking about what Jesus had just said.

"I must leave you," Jesus had said. "I must die on a cross and go back to God. But in a mysterious way, God and I will always be with each one of you."

What did Jesus mean? Peter wondered. How could he go away and still be with him?

Now Jesus spoke again. "I want joy for each one of you. And so I want you to obey a new rule. I want you to love one another, just as I love you."

Peter said aloud, "I don't always feel loving. Sometimes I get angry."

Jesus said, "You may not always feel loving, but I want you to love one another. That means that when you are angry, you give someone another chance. You forgive one another and you help one another."

James said, "But what will happen to us when you go?"

Jesus said, "You are my friends. I will always be your friend. I will always be with you, even if you can't see me."

Thomas did not understand what Jesus was saying, but he said, "I only want to do what you want me to do, Jesus."

"This is what I want you to do, my friends," said Jesus. "I want you to love one another. That is what I will always want my friends to do: love one another."

Ask:
■ What did Jesus say in today's story about love?

Teach children this rhythmic chant, stressing the bolded syllables:

Jesus **says**,
    love **one** a**noth**er;
This is **how**
    we **love** each **other**.

Consider adding clapping, knee-slapping or other sounds or movements to the chant. Practice the chant until children are comfortable saying it in unison.

After children have learned the chant, ask:
■ How do we show our love for the people in our families?

After children have shared several examples, recite the chant together. Repeat it for other examples of ways we love the people in our families.

Continue, if time allows, alternately chanting and sharing responses to these questions:
■ How do we show our love for our friends?
■ How do we show our love for the people here at church?
■ How do we show our love for Jesus?
■ How do we show our love for God?

Prayer:
■ Dear Jesus, thanks for teaching us to love each other. Help us to love each other, better and better. *Amen.*

Thank the children for joining you and invite them to return to their seats.

■ ■ ■ ■ ■

John 14:1-14

Jesus answered him, "I am the way, the truth, and the life; no one goes to the Father except by me." (John 14:6, *Today's English Version*)

Summary

In this reading from the Gospel of John, Jesus explains that knowing him results in knowing God. In today's homily, children first talk about losing their way, then hear today's story, and finally share the expectation that, wherever they go, Jesus will accompany them and lead them closer to God.

Materials

Bible

Homily

Invite the children to come forward for today's homily. Ask them to sit in a semicircle around you.

Discuss:
■ Did you ever lose your way?
■ What happened?
■ How did you feel?
■ Did anyone help you?
■ How did you find your way again?
■ Sometimes we feel afraid or uncertain about our own lives, just as if we had "lost our way."
■ When Jesus was ready to leave his friends, they felt afraid and uncertain, too.
■ Jesus comforted his friends. He made a promise to them. And that's the story I want to tell you today.

Hold the Bible open to the Gospel of John as you tell today's story:

Just before he died, Jesus was eating a last meal with his friends. Jesus looked at his friends; he loved them very much.

"I am going away," said Jesus. "Hard times are just ahead of us. Soon I will die."

The friends of Jesus were afraid. "Jesus, we don't want you to leave us," they said.

"Don't be afraid," said Jesus. His voice was strong and calm. "Trust in God. Trust in me, too. I am going to go to God, but I promise you that I will come back to you.

"I have to go away so that I can get a place ready for you, a place with God. This is what the place will be like: a wonderful house with many, many rooms. There will be room for each one of you to live with God."

Some of the friends looked even more worried. "Jesus," they said, "this is too hard for us to understand. How can we go to live with God?"

59

Jesus smiled. "You know the way to get to God!"

Thomas said, "I *don't* know. I don't even know where you are going, Jesus. How can I get there too?"

"Just trust in me," said Jesus. "I am the way to God. I will come to take you to God myself."

Discuss with the children:
- How did Jesus comfort his friends? What did he promise them?
- Jesus tells us that he is the way to God: if we follow Jesus, he will bring us to God.
- No matter where we go in life, no matter what we do, if we follow Jesus, he will bring us safely to God.

Invite children to imagine where they might go in life—literally, as in geographic places, or figuratively, as in what they plan to do as they grow older.

Prayer

Encourage children to pray aloud for the possible places they might go in life. Close by praying:
- Thank you, Jesus, for showing us the way to God. Help us to know that you are with us wherever we go. *Amen.*

Thank the children for joining you and invite them to return to their seats.

■ ■ ■ ■ ■

John 14:15-21

"I will ask the Father, and he will give you another Helper, who will stay with you forever. He is the Spirit, who reveals the truth about God." (John 14:16-17a, *Today's English Version***)**

Summary

In this reading from the Gospel of John, Jesus promises his followers the guidance and closeness of the Holy Spirit. In today's homily, children first discuss friendship, then listen to today's story about their relationship with the Holy Spirit.

Materials

Bible
pictures of friends printed at the end of today's homily (pp. 63-64.)

Before the homily cut out pages 63-64 along the dotted line.

Homily

Invite the children to come forward for today's homily. Ask the children to sit in a semicircle around you.

Show children the pictures of friends found at the end of today's homily. After showing each picture, ask:

■ What are these friends doing?
■ How do you think these friends feel today? Why?

After discussing both pictures, ask:
■ Who are our friends?
■ What can we do with our friends?
■ How do we feel when we are with our friends?

Explain that Jesus liked to spend time with his friends, too—as in today's story.

Hold the Bible open to the Gospel of Matthew as you tell today's story:

Jesus is with his friends.

Jesus shares bread and wine with his friends.

Jesus says, "I love you, my friends. I love you and God loves you, too. I am glad you are all my friends together.

"God will send you another friend. This friend is the Holy Spirit."

"Can we see the Holy Spirit?" ask Jesus' friends.

"No," says Jesus. "You cannot see the Holy Spirit."

"Can we touch the Holy Spirit?" ask Jesus' friends.

"No," says Jesus. "You cannot touch the Holy Spirit."

Then Jesus said, "But the Holy Spirit will always be with you. The Holy Spirit will help you know that I am always with you.

"You are my friends."

Or:

Ask the children to stand together in a circle. Sing and act out these verses to the tune of "If You're Happy and You Know It":

> If the Spirit lives in you, then
>   clap your hands. *(clap, clap)*
> If the Spirit lives in you, then
>   clap your hands. *(clap, clap)*
> If the Spirit lives in you,

You can tell the world good news.
If the Spirit lives in you, then clap your hands. *(clap, clap)*

Repeat with these additional verses:
- If the Spirit lives in you, then stomp your feet...
- If the Spirit lives in you, then hop and jump...
- If the Spirit lives in you, then spin around...

Invite the children to make up other verses and movement.

If you wish, discuss with the children:
- How is Jesus like our friends in church this morning?
- How is Jesus different from our friends in church this morning?
- How can we stay close to our friends?
- How can we stay close to Jesus?

Prayer

- Thank you, Jesus, for our friends. Thank you, Jesus, for being our friend. Thank you, Jesus, for sending our friend, the Holy Spirit. *Amen.*

Thank the children for joining you and invite them to return to their seats.

John 14:23-29

"Peace is what I leave with you; it is my own peace that I give you. I do not give it as the world does. Do not be worried and upset; do not be afraid."
(John 14:27, *Today's English Version*)

Summary

In this reading from the Gospel of John, Jesus promises his disciples both the Holy Spirit and deep, abiding peace. In today's homily, children act out a series of strong emotions, then hear the reassuring news that Jesus is with us, no matter how we feel.

Materials

Bible

Homily

Invite the children to come forward for today's homily. Stand in a circle with the children.

Say:
- I'm going to call out some feelings.
- I want us all to act out those feelings together.

Call out several feelings and encourage the children to act out the feelings together. For example, if you say "happy," children might jump up and down with big smiles on their faces. Let the children decide how they will act out each feeling.

If possible, encourage the children to lead the game by choosing feelings for the others to act out. If necessary, choose additional feelings from this list:
- tired
- worried
- angry
- peaceful
- friendly
- sad
- lonely
- proud
- frightened

End the activity by saying:
- Sometimes we feel good.
- Sometimes we feel mad or scared.
- No matter what we feel, someone is with us.
- Listen to today's story to find out who.

Ask the children to sit in a semicircle around you. Hold the Bible open to the Gospel of John as you tell today's story:

Jesus sat down to eat with his friends. "Soon I will go away," said Jesus. "But I will leave you two special gifts."

"A new boat?" asked Peter.

"A new pair of sandals?" asked James.

"A special treat to eat?" asked John.

"No," said Jesus. "You can't touch these gifts. You can't see these gifts. But you will feel these gifts in your heart."

The friends looked at each other. What kind of gifts was Jesus talking about?

"One gift will be God's own Spirit," said Jesus. "God's Spirit will come to you and teach you and help you. You won't see God's Spirit, but you will know how to follow my way—even when I'm gone."

"What is your other gift, Jesus?" asked Nathanael.

"Peace is my second gift," said Jesus. "Peace is what I leave with you. Even when you are worried or angry or afraid— even when you can't see me—I will be with you."

If you wish, discuss with the children:
■ When are you glad to know that Jesus is with you?

Prayer

■ Jesus, thanks for always being with us, even though we can't see you. Thanks for being close when we are worried or angry or afraid. *Amen.*

Thank the children for joining you and invite them to return to their seats.

66

John 15:1-8

"I am the vine, and you are the branches. Those who remain in me, and I in them, will bear much fruit; for you can do nothing without me."
(John 15:5, *Today's English Version*)

Summary

In this reading from the Gospel of John, Jesus teaches that he is "the real vine," in whose love we must remain if we are to grow and thrive. In today's homily, children hear today's story, then complete a poster reflecting their union with Jesus, their "vine."

Materials

Bible
thick yarn in shades of green
scissors
poster board
felt marker
glue

Before the homily, in a winding, vertical path down the center of the poster board, letter the name *Jesus.* Glue lengths of green yarn along, around and through the letters to form a thick, green vine.

Homily

Invite the children to come forward for today's homily. Ask them to sit in a semicircle around you.

Set up the poster so children can see it. Ask someone to read the name written on the poster: *Jesus.*

Hold the Bible open to the Gospel of John as you tell today's story:

A vine grows from the ground in spring. The sun shines on the vine. Rain waters the ground around the vine. A gardener takes care of the vine.

The vine grows tall and green. Branches grow from the vine, thick and sturdy. Flowers grow on the branches, and then sweet fruit.

The gardener is glad to see the sweet fruit grow on the branches of the vine.

Jesus says, "I am like a vine. I have many friends who stay as close to me as branches are to a vine."

Jesus says, "You are like branches, my friends. You need to stay close to one another and to me so you can have good things in your life, like the good fruit that grows on a branch."

Jesus says, "God is like a gardener. God takes care of me and of all the friends who stay close to me."

Jesus says, "I love you just as God loves me. Stay close to one other. Stay close to me. Stay close to God."

Discuss:
- What does Jesus call himself in today's gospel? (a vine)
- What is a vine?
- A vine can have branches, leaves and fruit attached it to it.
- Jesus says that he is like a vine; many people can be close to him.
- If we stay close to Jesus, he promises us that we will have "fruit"—good things—in our life. We will be able to know God's love, and to show it to others.
- Who do we know who stays close to Jesus?

Invite children to add to the vine poster branches for people they know who stay close to Jesus. Children glue on one yarn "branch" for each person, naming the people as they add each branch.

Cut an extra length of yarn for each child, and invite the children each to add one additional branch— representing themselves—to the poster.

Prayer
- Dear Jesus, help us to remain close to you, as close as branches are to their vine. *Amen.*

Thank the children for joining you and invite them to return to their seats.

■ ■ ■ ■ ■

John 15:9-17

"My commandment is this: love one another, just as I love you. And you are my friends if you do what I command you." (John 15:12, 14, *Today's English Version*)

Summary

In this reading from the Gospel of John, Jesus gives the greatest of all commandments, to love one another. In today's homily, children hear today's story, then discuss rules, including the most important rule, love.

Materials

Bible
large sheet of poster board on which you have drawn a large, red heart
broad-tip felt marker

Homily

Invite the children to come forward for today's homily. Ask the children to sit in a semicircle around you.

Hold the Bible open to the Gospel of John as you tell today's story:

Jesus looked around the table. How he loved these good friends who broke bread with him: noisy John and James, brave Thomas, Peter, who always said just what he thought, and so many others.

But all his friends looked puzzled and worried right now. They were thinking about what Jesus had just said.

"I must leave you," Jesus had said. "I must die on a cross and go back to God. But in a mysterious way, God and I will always be with each one of you."

What did Jesus mean? Peter wondered. How could he go away and still be with him?

Now Jesus spoke again. "I want joy for each one of you. And so I want you to obey a new rule. I want you to love one another, just as I love you."

Peter said aloud, "I don't always feel very loving. Sometimes I get angry at people."

Jesus said, "You may not always feel loving, but I want you to

love one another. That means that when you are angry, you give someone another chance. You forgive one another and you help one another."

James said, "But what will happen to us when you go?"

Jesus said, "You are my friends. I will always be your friend. I will always be with you, even if you can't see me."

Thomas did not understand what Jesus was saying, but he said, "I only want to do what you want me to do, Jesus."

"This is what I want you to do, my friends," said Jesus. "I want you to love one another. That is what I will always want my friends to do: love one another."

Ask the children:
- What is a rule?
- What rules do we have at home? at school? here in church?
- What are some rules that you do not like? Why don't you like these rules?
- What are some rules that you think are very important? Why do you think these are good rules?

Show children the poster with the heart. Say:
- In today's gospel story, Jesus tells his friends about a very important rule. Who can tell me what that rule is? *(Love each other.)*
- That's right, Jesus tells us to love each other!

In large letters across the heart on the poster write:
- Love each other!

Continue:
- Now tell me, how can we love our brothers and sisters? our moms and dads? our grandmothers and grandfathers? our friends? the other children with us right now?
- How can we love people who are hungry? those who have no homes and must live on the street? people who are sick? people who are sad?

Invite children to repeat several times in unison the phrase printed on the poster:

- Love each other!

Prayer

- Jesus, this is the best of all rules: Love each other! Help us to do just that. *Amen.*

Thank the children for joining you and invite them to return to their seats.

John 16:5-15

**"All that my Father has is mine; that is
why I said that the Spirit will take
what I give him and tell it to you."
(John 16:15, *Today's English Version*)**

Summary

In this reading from the Gospel
of John, Jesus tells of the coming
Helper, the Holy Spirit, revealing
something of the nature of our
Triune God. The concept of the
Trinity is a tough one for adults to
grasp, let alone children. In today's
homily, children hear today's
gospel story, then briefly explore
the Trinity in its broadest terms,
identifying the myriad ways in
which they experience God in
their lives.

Materials

Bible
several Trinitarian symbols, for
    example, a triangle cut from
    cardboard, a drawing of three
    interlocking rings, a shamrock,
    etc.

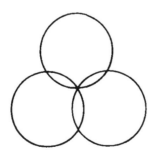

Homily

Invite the children to come forward for today's homily. Ask them
to sit in a semicircle around you.

Hold the Bible open to the Gospel
of John as you tell today's story:

**Jesus sat at supper with his
friends. Jesus gave his friends
a new rule. He said, "I want you
to love one another as I have
loved you."**

**Jesus promised his friends two
gifts. He promised them peace,
even when times were hard,
and he promised them a
Helper.**

**Jesus said, "I have many things
I want to tell you; so many
things I want to teach you. But I
can't, not now. Soon I must go."**

**"But Jesus," said Thomas, "How
will we be able to do what you
want if you don't teach us these
things?"**

**"I will send you a Helper," said
Jesus. "The Holy Spirit will be
your Helper. The Spirit will
teach you about God. The Spirit
will teach you about me."**

71

"Thank you, Jesus!" said Peter. "The Spirit will teach us what God wants."

"Thank you, Jesus!" said James. "The Spirit will teach us what you want."

And do you know what happened? The Helping Spirit came, just as Jesus had promised. The Spirit came like wind and fire.

"Praise God," said the friends of Jesus. "The Spirit teaches us the great things of God!"

"Praise Jesus," said the friends. "He has sent us the Spirit as he promised!"

"Praise the Spirit," said the friends. "The Helper has come to live with us forever!"

Pass around the trinitarian symbols for children to hold and examine. Ask:
■ Have you heard the word *Trinity?* What can you tell us about the Trinity?
■ The Trinity is another name for God. The word *trinity* comes from the number three. God is sometimes called "the Trinity" because we think of God as three persons—God the Father, God the Son (Jesus) and God the Holy Spirit.

Acknowledge that understanding the Trinity is a hard thing. Most people spend a lifetime trying to understand. Invite the children to begin that process:
■ We come to know God the Father through the wonderful world that God created:
— What can we learn about God in a noisy thunderstorm? in waves at the ocean? in a peaceful summer evening? in rain or snow?
— What can we learn about God in a beautiful painting? wonderful music? a poem or a story?
■ We come to know God the Son—Jesus—through the stories God gives us in the Bible:
— What are your favorite stories about Jesus?
— What are your favorite words of Jesus?
■ We come to know God the Holy Spirit through the love that people show for us:
— How does God show God's love for us through our parents? our grandparents? our brothers and sisters?
— How does God show God's love for us through people at church? at your school? in your neighborhood?

Prayer

■ Thank you for our time together, God—God, Jesus and the Holy Spirit. Thank you for being with us when we are together and when we are apart. *Amen.*

Thank the children for joining you and invite them to return to their seats.

John 17:1-11

"I pray...for those you gave me...."
(John 17:6a, *Today's English Version*)

Summary

In this reading from the Gospel of John, Jesus prays for his friends, his disciples and followers. In today's homily, children hear this story, then reflect on the people in their lives by whom they feel loved.

Materials

Bible
large sheet of poster board
felt marker

Homily

Invite the children to come forward for today's homily. Ask them to sit in a semicircle around you.

Can you name people who love and care for you? You name the people and I'll write their names on this sheet of poster board. (If you have plenty of time, you might choose to have the children draw pictures of people who love and care for them.)

Invite children to name people who love and care for them. If they need help, you might suggest:

- family members living at home
- family members living someplace else
- teachers or daycare workers
- neighbors
- friends
- pastors and others at church

Say:
- Jesus loved and cared for his friends, too. And Jesus' friends loved and cared for him.
- Let's listen to a story about Jesus and his friends.

Hold the Bible open to the Gospel of John as you tell today's story:

On the night before he died, Jesus ate a special meal with his friends. He told them that he would die. He told them that God would give him new life.

His friends had many questions. Jesus had many answers to their questions, but the most important answer was that God loved them.

"Yes," his friends said at last. "We believe that you come from God. We trust you now."

"I have told you all this so that you will be brave during the hard time that is coming," Jesus said. "Remember: I won't really be alone during this hard time. God is always with me."

After Jesus finished saying this, he looked up to heaven and prayed to God, "Father, the time has come for me to die. Give

me strength and courage, so that I may give glory to you. I have shown your glory on earth; I have finished the work you gave me to do.

"I have told all my friends about you. You gave me these friends, and they are your children, too. They have listened to my words about you. They know I come from you. They know about your love.

"Soon I will be with you Holy Father! When I am gone, be close to them. Help them to love and care for each other, so that others will learn about you because of them."

When Jesus finished praying, he looked around at his friends. "I love you all," he said. "I need you to love and care for me now. I want you to always love and care for each other, too."

Review with children the names they added to the poster of people who love and care for them. Ask:
■ What do these people do when we feel sad? when we feel hurt? when we feel happy? when we want to learn something new?
■ Jesus knew how important it is to have people who care for and love us. Jesus knew how important it is for us to care for and love others.
■ Jesus gives us one another to love and care for each other. When do we feel especially loved and cared for?
■ What are new ways we could love and care for each other?

Encourage the children to suggest a variety of answers to that last question. If no one else suggests *listening to one another* and *praying for one another,* suggest these answers yourself. Invite children to listen to one another, and then pray for one another in today's closing prayer.

Prayer

Ask each child to suggest something he or she would like another child to pray for.

After each suggestion, ask another child to immediately pray for that request. For example, if one child says, "Pray for my grandma, who can't see very well," ask another child to immediately pray for that child's grandmother: "I pray that Jason's grandma will be able to see better."

Allow children to pass if they don't feel comfortable praying aloud. Some children may feel more comfortable if offered a simple prayer form to use, for example:
■ Jesus, please help... *(In our example, "Jesus, please help...Jason's grandma.")*
■ Jesus, thank you for...

Conclude the prayer by praying:
■ Jesus, we're glad so many friends loved and cared for you. Thank you for the people who love and care for us. *Amen.*

Thank the children for joining you and invite them to return to their seats.

■ ■ ■ ■ ■

John 17:11b-19

"Holy Father! Keep them safe by the power of your name, the name you gave me, so that they may be one just as you and I are one. While I was with them, I kept them safe by the power of your name, the name you gave me. I protected them..." (John 17:11b-12a, *Today's English Version*)

Summary

In this reading from the Gospel of John, Jesus prays for his disciples, that God may grant them safety, unity, joy and commitment. In today's homily, children listen as Jesus prays for them, then discuss times when they would like Jesus to keep them safe.

Materials

Bible
several pictures of potentially scary places or events, for example, a beach with big waves washing ashore, a dense forest, a deserted street at night, a lightning storm, a large snarling dog, etc.

Homily

Invite the children to come forward for today's homily. Ask them to sit in a semicircle around you.

Begin the homily by saying:
■ Did you know that the Bible

tells about a time when Jesus prayed for you?
■ It's true, and that's the story I want to tell you today.

Hold the Bible open to the Gospel of John as you tell today's story:

One day, Jesus was with his friends, his disciples. They were having a special meal together, the last meal Jesus would have with them before he died.

Jesus prayed to God at this last meal with his friends. He prayed that God would help all his friends, *including each of us here this morning*.

Let's close our eyes and listen as Jesus prays:

"Holy Father, thank you for always being close to me, at any time of the day, wherever I am.

"Holy Father, I pray for every one of these followers of mine,

75

big or small, old or young, adults, teenagers or children.

"I pray that you will keep them safe. Protect them during all the scary times they will face.

"I pray that you will make them one, always loving each other, even when it's hard to get along.

"I pray that you will have as much joy as I have, always delighting in the beauty of your world and the love you give them.

"I pray that they will always love you, always trust you, always turn to you for help.

"Thank you, Holy Father, for loving us all so much."

And then Jesus said, "Amen."

Invite children to open their eyes. Discuss:
■ What did Jesus ask God to do for us? *(Accept all answers from children. If no child mentions safety, mention it yourself.)*
■ Jesus prayed that God would keep us safe.

One at a time, hold up the "scary" pictures and ask:
■ What is this a picture of?
■ Would you feel a little bit frightened if you were in this place? *(Phrase this question to reflect the content of the picture being displayed.)*
■ What would you need in order to feel safe in this place?

Repeat these questions for each picture. Remember that what might be scary for one child may not be scary to another child. Affirm the legitimacy of each child's feelings and do not try to talk them out of their fears.

Continue:
■ Jesus knew we would have scary times, so he asked God to keep us safe and protect us in all the scary times.

Hold up each picture again. As you hold up each picture, ask these questions:
■ Would God be with us here (or in this situation)?
■ How might God help to keep us safe in this scary place (or situation)?

Prayer

■ Jesus, thank you for remembering us in your prayers. Thank you, God, for being with us in every scary time and place. *Amen.*

Thank the children for joining you and invite them to return to their seats.

John 17:20-26

"I pray that they may all be one. Father! May they be in us, just as you are in me, and I am in you. May they be one, so that the world will believe that you sent me." (John 17:21, *Today's English Version*)

Summary

In this reading from the Gospel of John, Jesus prays for the unity of future believers. In today's homily, children first sing a familiar camp song, then use the song as a refrain in today's story. An optional song concludes the homily.

Materials

Bible
optional:
pianist to accompany the children (and the parishioners) as they learn and sing "I Have a Family," printed below

Homily

Invite the children to come forward for today's homily. Ask them to sit in a semicircle around you.

With the children, sing the old summer-camp and preschool favorite, "The More We Get Together":

> The more we get together,
>   together, together,
> The more we get together,
>   the happier we'll be.

> For my friends are your friends,
>   and your friends are my
>   friends.
> The more we get together,
>   the happier we'll be.

Explain that today's Bible story is about getting together with friends and with God.

Hold the Bible open to the Gospel of John as you tell today's story. Lead the children in singing "The More We Get Together" as a story refrain where indicated:

Jesus ate supper
    with women and men.
Each one there
    was a special friend.
(Sing "The More We Get Together.")

Then Jesus said
    a special prayer
For his special friends
    gathered there.

"Father," he prayed,
    "I'm your Son.
You sent me here.
    Now my work is done.
(Sing "The More We Get Together.")

77

"These are my sisters
    and brothers you see.
God, we're all members
    of your family.

"Dear God, keep
    your family close together;
keep them close
    forever and ever."
*(Sing "The More We Get
Together.")*

If you wish, teach children (and the parishioners) the song "I Have a Family," printed below.

Prayer

■ Dear God, thanks for making all of us here into one, big family. *Amen.*

Thank the children for joining you and invite them to return to their seats.

I HAVE A FAMILY

Words and music by Pamela L. Hughes

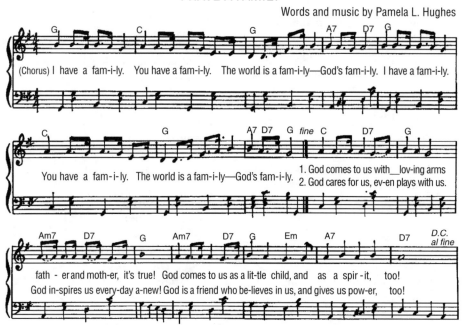

John 18:33-37

Jesus said, "My kingdom does not belong to this world... " (John 18:36a, 37b, *Today's English Version*)

Summary

In this reading from the Gospel of John, Pilate interrogates Jesus on the nature of Jesus' "kingdom." In today's homily, children take turns pretending to be kings and queens, then hear a rhymed version of today's story.

Materials

1 sheet of 12" x 18" yellow construction paper or thin cardboard
scissors
crayons or felt pens
clear tape or stapler
optional:
glue in squirt bottles
glitter
scraps of colored tissue paper
sequins

Before the homily create a child-sized crown to be worn by the children in today's homily, using the crown pattern printed below. Enlarge the pattern on a sheet of yellow construction paper or thin cardboard.

Make a circle with the crown and tape or staple the ends together. (At this point, you may want to size the crown to a child's head.) If you wish, decorate the crown with glitter, scraps or colored tissue paper, sequins, etc.

Homily

Invite the children to come forward for today's homily. Ask them to sit in a semicircle around you.

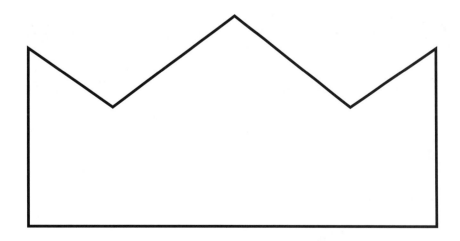

Show children the crown you created **before the homily.** Discuss:
- What do I have here?
- That's right, it's a crown. Who wears crowns?
- That's right, kings and queens sometimes wear crowns.
- Kings and queens are the rulers (or leaders or bosses) over many people.
- Good kings and queens try to help the people they rule or lead.

Invite the children to stand together in a circle. Ask a volunteer to be the first king or queen. Place the crown on the king or queen's head. The king or queen wears the crown while asking the other children to join him or her in doing one or two simple movements. Movement examples:
- clapping
- hopping
- hugging

After about 10 seconds of movement, ask a new volunteer to be the next king or queen.

Use simple comments to emphasize that the king or queen is leading the children; the children are following the king or queen. After five or six kings and queens have led the children in movements, ask the children to be seated. Explain that today's story is about a special king.

You can place the crown in sight of the children to serve as a visual focus for today's story. Hold the Bible open to the Gospel of John as you tell today's story:

When Jesus rides to Jerusalem town,
He wears no robes, he wears no crown.

But the people know that he's our king.
"Hosanna, Jesus," they shout and sing.

Jesus hears, but his head bows down.
Hard times wait in Jerusalem town.

Soldiers search for Jesus by night.
They drag him to the palace by morning's light.

The governor asks, "Are you a king?
Is it true what your people shout and sing?

"Here you stand without a crown.
Do you think you can rule in Jerusalem town?"

Jesus says, "I need no crown.
I will not rule in Jerusalem town.

"I speak God's truth. I show God's love.
That's why I was sent by God above."

Without any soldiers, without any crown,
King Jesus stands in Jerusalem town.

Prayer

- King Jesus, we love and follow you. *Amen.*

Thank the children for joining you and invite them to return to their seats.

John 20:1-9

Early on Sunday morning, while it was still dark, Mary Magdalene went to the tomb and saw that the stone had been taken away from the entrance. (John 20:1, *Today's English Version*)

Summary

In this reading from the Gospel of John, Mary, Peter and John discover Jesus' empty tomb. In today's homily, children hear the story, then imagine themselves present in the garden as they realize for the first time: Jesus is alive!

Materials

Bible

Homily

Invite the children to come forward for today's homily. Ask them to sit in a semicircle around you.

Hold the Bible open to the Gospel of John as you tell today's story:

Very early in the morning, while it was still very quiet and very dark, Mary walked across town to the cemetery. She felt sad. Every now and then she sighed. Two days ago, on the darkest, most painful day of Mary's life, her good friend Jesus was killed.

Head down, gray with grief, Mary shuffled through the dirt.

I miss him so much, she thought.

Finally, at the entrance to the cemetery, she stopped and looked up. "God," she prayed, "comfort me. Comfort all of Jesus' friends."

She headed for Jesus' tomb. She stopped. She gasped. She began to tremble. What was this? The stone at the entrance to Jesus' tomb was moved aside.

Mary ran, back through the dusty, dark streets. She pounded on the door of Peter's house. "Peter, Peter," she cried, trying to catch her breath, "come quickly...to the tomb...he's gone!"

Peter and John ran back with Mary. John got there first and went in. Just as Mary had said, Jesus' body was not there. The strips of cloth that they had wrapped around Jesus after he died were neatly folded and lying on the bare stone where they had placed Jesus' body.

Then Peter arrived and walked into the tomb, too. "He's alive,"

Peter whispered. "Jesus is alive. I know it."

Invite children to imagine that they are with Mary, who finds the tomb empty on the first Easter morning:

- You are there in the quiet darkness of early morning. The ground is cold and damp with dew. All is silent.
- You find the tomb where you know your friend Jesus is buried. How do you feel? sad? nervous?
- Then you hear the good news. Jesus is not dead, he's alive! Now how do you feel? What will you tell your friends? your family?
- Let's pretend that all the other people seated in church this morning have not yet heard the good news that Jesus is alive!

- What would we like to tell them?

Let children turn to and address the parishioners with the good news of Jesus' resurrection. Encourage a variety of announcements from children. You can encourage differing responses with suggestions such as:

- Why is this such good news?
- How do you feel knowing that Jesus is alive?

Prayer

- Jesus, we celebrate your resurrection. You are alive! Good news! *Amen.*

Thank the children for joining you and invite them to return to their seats.

■ ■ ■ ■ ■

John 20:19-23

Jesus said to them again, "Peace be with you. As the Father sent me, so I send you." Then he breathed on them and said, "Receive the Holy Spirit." (John 20:21-22, *Today's English Version*)

Summary

In this reading from the Gospel of John, the resurrected Jesus appears to the frightened disciples and grants them his peace and the Holy Spirit. In today's homily, children hear this story, then discuss the "gift" of the Holy Spirit.

Materials

Bible

large box brightly wrapped in gift wrap and ribbon, to which is attached a large gift tag reading *To All My Children, Love, Jesus*

Homily

Invite the children to come forward for today's homily. Ask them to sit in a semicircle around you.

Hold the Bible open to the Gospel of John as you tell today's story:

Early on Sunday morning, Mary went to the cave where Jesus' friends had laid his body. The huge stone that had covered the doorway had been rolled away.

But when Mary looked inside the cave, it was empty! Mary ran to Simon Peter and Jesus' other friends and said, "They have taken the Lord from the tomb and we don't know where he is!" Peter and the other friends ran to the tomb. Empty!

Now Mary stood outside crying.

A man said to her, "Why are you crying?" The man called her by name: "Mary!"

Then she cried, "Teacher!" She held out her arms to him. It was Jesus—no longer dead, but alive.

Late that evening the friends were together in a room with heavy, locked doors.

Suddenly, even though the doors had not opened, Jesus was there—right in the room! He said, "Peace be with you."

"It's Jesus!" said his friends. They leapt up with joy to see him. They stared in amazement at the marks that the soldiers had made in his hands and side when they killed him.

Jesus said, "As I breathe on each of you, I give you the Holy Spirit." The friends felt the breath of Jesus on them like a breeze. "I give you the Spirit and I send you out," said Jesus. "Do my work. Tell my good news."

Show children the large "gift" prepared before the session. Ask:
■ What is this?
■ How would you feel if someone gave you a box like this?
■ If you received a box like this, what would you hope might be inside it?

Ask an older child to come forward and to read aloud the tag hanging on the "gift": *To All My Children, Love, Jesus.* Discuss:
■ In today's story, we heard about a special gift that Jesus gives.

What is that special gift? *(the Holy Spirit)*
■ To whom does Jesus give this special gift, the Holy Spirit? *(Be certain that the children understand that they, too, have been given the Spirit.)*
■ Who is the Holy Spirit? What does the Holy Spirit do? *(Many answers are possible here: leads and guides us, helps us speak about God; comforts and consoles us; teaches us about God; helps us to talk with God; etc.)*
■ Where is the Holy Spirit? Can we see the Holy Spirit? touch the Holy Spirit? *(Encourage children to understand that, though not visible, the Holy Spirit is a constant companion and friend.)*

Prayer

Invite children to offer spontaneous prayers to the Holy Spirit, for example:
■ Thanks, Holy Spirit, for being here with me right now.
■ Holy Spirit, help me to follow Jesus.

Thank the children for joining you and invite them to return to their seats.

John 20:24-31

Thomas said, "Unless I see the scars of the nails in his hands and put my finger on those scars and my hand in his side, I will not believe." (John 20:25b, *Today's English Version*)

Summary

In this reading from the Gospel of John, Thomas touches the risen Jesus and affirms that Jesus is his Lord and his God. In today's homily, children explore touch, then hear today's gospel story.

Materials

Bible
assorted materials and objects demonstrating different tactile sensations, for example, a smooth piece of wood, a piece of rough bark, sand paper, cotton balls, smooth and ridged uncooked pasta shapes, feather, plastic cup, sponge, golf ball, metal spoon, eraser, etc.

Homily

Invite the children to come forward for today's homily. Ask them to sit in a semicircle around you.

Spread the materials and objects in front of the children and invite them to touch. As they touch, discuss:
■ How do all these different things feel? Which feel smooth? rough? sticky? soft? hard?

■ Which do you like to touch? not like to touch?
■ Besides what we are touching here, what else do you like to touch? not like to touch?

After a minute or two of discussion, say:
■ Touch was once very important to a friend of Jesus, and that's the story I want to tell you today.

Hold the Bible open to the Gospel of John as you tell today's story:

Remember how Jesus died on a cross?

That was a sad day. Jesus' friends hugged each other and cried.

One friend, Mary, went to the tomb. But the tomb was empty. Jesus was gone!

Mary ran to Jesus' other friends. "Jesus is gone!"

"Where is he?" said all Jesus' friends. "Where's Jesus?" *(Peer around the room. Some child may well call out, "Here's Jesus!" If so, take advantage of it: "Yes, here's Jesus!")*

Suddenly Jesus was right there. "Peace be with you," said Jesus. All the friends talked to Jesus. "Jesus, you were dead!" they said.

"Yes," said Jesus. "I did die, but now I live." Then Jesus was gone—*(snap fingers or clap hands)*—just like that.

Another friend of Jesus, Thomas, came. All Jesus' friends said to him, "Thomas! Jesus is alive! We saw Jesus!"

"Oh no!" said Thomas. "I can't believe that! I *won't* believe that, not unless I can touch Jesus myself!"

Then just like that—*(snap fingers or clap hands)*—Jesus was there.

And Jesus said, "Touch me, Thomas. See for yourself! I'm really alive!"

Thomas touched Jesus. *(Invite children to hold out their palms and touch one another, just as Thomas touched Jesus.)*

"You *are* Jesus," said Thomas. "You *are* alive. Jesus, you are my God."

If you wish, discuss with the children:
- Why do you think Thomas wanted to touch Jesus?
- When have we really wanted to touch someone? to have someone touch us?
- When in church do we touch each other?

Prayer

- Jesus, thanks for the gift of touch. Thanks for using touch to convince Thomas that you really, truly were alive. *Amen.*

Thank the children for joining you and invite them to return to their seats. As they head back to join their friends and families, invite all of the parishioners to exchange a handshake or hug...a holy touch.

■ ■ ■ ■ ■

John 21:1-14

**As the sun was rising, Jesus
stood at the water's edge, but
the disciples did not know that
it was Jesus. (John 21:4,
Today's English Version)**

Summary

In this reading from the Gospel of
John, Jesus makes another post-res-
urrection appearance to the disciples, directing them to a large
catch of fish. In today's homily,
children first hear this story, then
help retell the story, exploring how
Jesus cares for them, day by day.

Materials

Bible

Homily

Invite the children to come forward for today's homily. Ask them
to sit in a semicircle around you.

Hold the Bible open to the Gospel
of John as you tell today's story:

**Jesus had died. Jesus had risen.
Jesus had shown himself to his
friends.**

Then Jesus had gone away.

**One day, Peter said, "I'm going
fishing."**

**"We'll go with you," his friends
said.**

**They went out in a boat and
fished all night—but caught
nothing.**

**As the sun rose, they saw a man
standing at the water's edge. He
said, "Haven't you caught anything?"**

"Not a thing," they said.

**Then the man said, "Throw
your net out on the right side
of the boat—you'll catch some
fish!"**

**The friends looked again at the
man on shore. "It's Jesus!" they
said.**

**"Jesus!" cried Peter. "My
teacher! My best friend!" He
jumped right into the water and
swam ashore.**

**There was Jesus, building a fire
on the sand. "Peter!" he
laughed. "Come and eat!"**

87

The others rowed to shore, pulling the net full of fish. Jesus cooked some fish and gave it to his friends with bread. "It's really Jesus!" the friends whispered, between bites of bread and fish. "Jesus is alive and with us again!"

Invite the children to pretend that they are fishing with the disciples on the sea of Galilee. Ask:
- Feel the boat rock back and forth? Feel the warm sun on our faces? Feel the rough wood of the sides of the boat? What else do you feel?
- Smell the salty water? Smell the fish? What else do you smell?
- Hear the sea gulls crying? Hear the waves hitting the side of the boat? What else do you hear?

Invite children into today's story:
- I feel frustrated because we've been fishing all day and have not caught one fish! How about you?
- There's someone on the shore, calling to us. What's he saying?
- Let's try putting the net on the other side. Oh, my! What's happening?

- Who do you think that man on the shore is? Who helped us get all these fish?

Invite children to describe ways in which Jesus helps them every day, like he helped the disciples. If children need help coming up with ideas, discuss:
- Sometimes Jesus helps us remember ways to help others, like sharing our toys, telling someone about Jesus or saying "I'm sorry." What has Jesus helped you do for others lately?
- Sometimes Jesus gives us the things we need each day, like sleep, food, a home and people who love us. What has Jesus given you lately?

Prayer

- Jesus, thanks for helping the disciples find the fish they needed. Thank you for giving us family and friends, food and clothing, love and caring. *Amen.*

Thank the children for joining you and invite them to return to their seats.